# CRAIL AND ITS FISHERIES
# 1550–1600

# CRAIL AND ITS FISHERIES
# 1550–1600

# THOMAS RIIS

# Contents

# Foreword

This most welcome book is the fruit of several years labour by Professor Riis on the burgh court books of Crail and related records. It represents the most detailed study yet of any branch of 16th-century Scottish trade, involving fishermen and mariners sailing to the wild seas of the north and west of Scotland in the stormy months of autumn, and returning before Christmas with herring and cod for sale within Scotland, or destined for markets in England, France and the Baltic. The boats they sailed in were crears, half decked vessels of up to 30 tons, that could carry two yawls which did most of the actual fishing. The crears could also carry enough salt for a preliminary cure of the herring; or they could serve as cargo boats and take fully cured fish or other goods on to markets abroad, and perhaps return from Norway with wood for the herring barrels and other purposes. Crail was proba-bly the main fishing centre in the Firth of Forth at this time, but it was not the only one; many of the little burghs of Fife and Lothian joined in, and sometimes as many as 100 crears could be seen in harbour in Aberdeen on their way to and from the fishing.

As Professor Riis shows, the trade involved highly skilled and daring skippers, the 'contractors', who conducted the fishing with the help of other seamen fishermen, and merchants who commissioned these voyages and sold the fish received. Also essential to the trade were the coopers who made the barrels.

We tend to think of the burgesses of the old Scottish burghs as being jealous of privilege and strict in their rules about who may or may not profit from their position, and so they were. But this did not rule out enterprise and flexibility; coopers and skippers are also sometimes found as merchants on their own account, and merchants could operate in a variety of ways either as partners or as sole traders, sometimes helping to fit out the boats with salt and barrels, sometimes simply lending money. The profits they could make were high, but so were the risks they ran, so a wise merchant might spread his activity over several boats. Most of the merchants were burgesses of Crail itself, but capital was also attracted from other towns, especially from the merchants of Edinburgh.

The value of this study lies above all in its careful detail; never before has the business world of Scotland before the Union of the Crowns been exposed to such scrutiny, and we come away with admiration for the implicit bravery and skill of the mariners who could command such seas, and the ingenuity and enterprise of the merchants on shore who commissioned the sailors and traded the fish. Scotland in the century of the Reformation was not all wild preachers and vain nobility.

T. C. Smout
Chairman, Strathmartine Trust

# Preface and Acknowledgements

During my research on Scottish-Danish relations *c* 1450-1707,[1] I discovered an important number of fishing contracts in the burgh court books of Crail, which have survived (with gaps) for the period 1552-91. Many years later, Professor T C Smout encouraged me to study the contracts and Crail's fisheries in general in the second half of the 16th century. Generously, the Strathmartine Trust granted me three periods of work, during which I could stay at the Strathmartine Centre, St Andrews, in February-March 2005, in September 2014 and for two weeks in the spring of 2015.

Several institutions facilitated my research: the staff of the University Libraries of St Andrews and Kiel, of the National Library of Scotland at Edinburgh and of the Royal Library of Copenhagen, as well as those of the City Archives of Dundee and Edinburgh, of the National Archives of Scotland, Edinburgh, and of the National Archives (Rigsarkivet) of Copenhagen.

Granting me free accommodation at the Strathmartine Centre, the Strathmartine Trust offered me ideal conditions of work. The Centre's Director, Dr Barbara Crawford, and its secretaries were ever ready to sort out practical problems, which meant that I could fully concentrate on my research. Some historical problems I have discussed with Dr Crawford, with Dr Robert Smart, sometime Keeper of University Muniments, St Andrews, and above all with Professor T C Smout, who followed my work through the years, suggested my consultation of certain works, and read my manuscript, sharpening up my English and proposing improvements. Again my gratitude goes to the Strathmartine Trust that proposed to publish my research in its series of publications. To them all, the staffs of the institutions, Dr Crawford and her family, Dr Smart, Professor Smout and his family my most sincere gratitude: they made me feel fully at home during my stays in Scotland – Auld Acquaintance was not forgot.

Scottish fishing before the 18-19th centuries is known mainly from the usual sources, but these do not show us its organisation. However, ethnological studies help us to understand the burgh court books' scattered information on fishing techniques. The results of my investigation are divided into five chapters. In the first the preparations for the voyage are treated as far as barrels, salt and equipment were concerned. If not otherwise mentioned, the pound is the £Scots.

The second discusses the fishing grounds and their seasons. The third deals with the kinds of fish caught (mainly herring) and the fishing methods employed. An attempt is made to calculate the quantities caught; the burgh court books register the contracts obliging the contractors to deliver a certain quantity of fish by a certain date, whereas the customs accounts give the quantities actually declared. The fourth treats the economic aspects of the fisheries including the raising of working capital. The cost of production of a last of herring is calculated. As its estimated value is known from the contracts, the gross profits can be seen for certain years, both as far as the investment in the fisheries and in international (Baltic) trade in herring is concerned. In this context, the question of indemnities and interests is also discussed.

The fifth describes the groups of persons involved in the fisheries: the contractors who would receive a working capital from a merchant to pay back some months later in fish, and the merchants who would seldom sail themselves. The coopers form a particular group; sometimes they organised voyages to Norway to fetch timber and a few even engaged in the herring fisheries themselves.

Thomas Riis
St Andrews, May 2015

# Introduction

Whereas fishing for cod and its relatives is documented since the Viking Age, the herring fisheries in Northern Scotland are of medieval origin.[2] About 1400 the migrations of the herring changed direction, as the northern herring did not enter the Baltic, but remained in the North Sea.[3] Consequently, the fishing for herring in the North Sea increased; in 1491 Scottish herring was exported to England, France, the Netherlands, and Italy.[4] Initially, Scottish herring fisheries were concentrated in the southern firths, but by the 15th century herring was also taken off the coasts of Western Scotland.[5] For the Low Countries also herring played a role in international trade between the Baltic, Western France, Spain and Portugal. As the Netherlands could not feed themselves with corn, it had to be imported from the Baltic region (the so-called 'mother trade'), and herring was one of the articles furnished by the Dutch in return.[6]

At the beginning of the 15th century, Dutch fishing was undertaken by owners of small ships which depended on brokers for furnishing working capital and for the sale of the fish. By the middle of the century the brokers had become ship-owners themselves and cooperated with the skippers as partners. Consequently the fishermen became paid workers.[7]

In the course of the 15th century the Dutch herring fisheries were reorganized. Bigger vessels, the so-called 'buss' were used, which allowed the catch to be provisionally processed on board. Swift ships took the cured herring to packing enterprises on land and took back to the buss empty barrels, salt (mainly French or from the Iberian Peninsula) as well as victuals.[8] As herring must be processed within 48 hours of the catch,[9] the provisional cure on board represented a clear advantage over the traditional fishing method. Scottish, English and Irish fishermen cured their catch on the shore, whereas the French and the Dutch processed the fish on board.[10] Here the herring was gutted, salted and put into barrels, but as it shrinks, it had to be packed anew on land. Thus a fresh last of herring would hold 14 barrels, which would make a repacked final last of 12 barrels. For that reason a last of barrels would be reckoned as 14 barrels.[11]

The buss was a standard type of vessel; in the early 16th century it had three masts and a full deck and could load 60 tons or 30 lasts (the term last can also be used as a measure of shipping displacement where one last equals two tuns burden). Its crew numbered 12 to 15 men including coopers and picklers.[12] A Flemish description of 1547 mentions the buss as a vessel of 22-24 lasts with a round prow, they were good carriers of cargoes, but their sailing qualities could have been better.[13] Obviously, the buss fishing was more efficient, but it needed more capital than the traditional method. For that reason Scottish fishing could in the 19th century outrival the buss fishing by processing the herring on land.[14] The herring fisheries were seasonal activities. For the Dutch the season began on 24 June and lasted to the end of the year; in 1604 this period was extended to include January as well. The fishing began off Shetland and moved gradually towards the south in order to finish at Great Yarmouth.[15]

In the 15th century Scotland was also aware of the economic possibilities in the herring fisheries. Between 1424 and 1555 Parliament passed a number of statutes on herring fishing, on the construction of fishing vessels, and on the control of the product's quality. As far as fishing in the sea was concerned, the main legislation belongs to the 16th century. In 1584, Leith, Crail, Dumbarton and Ayr were recognized as staple herring ports.[16] Since 1573 fish could only be landed in a royal burgh; for a couple of years about 1580 fish taken in the Firth of Forth could be landed only at Crail or at Leith, but this rule was abolished in 1585. It was more important that since 1497 Scotland reserved the coastal zone for her own fishermen. The limit was fixed as 17 miles or a 'landkenning', ie the distance at which land can be seen from the top of the mast.[17]

In spite of quality control Scottish herring was not considered to be of the best quality. Towards the end of 1577 four categories of herring fetched different prices in France, among which Scottish and coastal herring were the cheapest quality (Table 1). In spite of this, France appears to have been the greatest foreign market for Scottish herring, but the Baltic region was also important.[18]

Fishing depends on the seasons; at the beginning of the 17th century we find the following scheme for fishermen based on the Forth:[19]

**March – May**
Cod fishing off Orkney, return home with salted and dried fish ('klipfisk', 'bacalao')

**Beginning of June – end of July**
Herring fishing off Shetland

**Augus – beginning of September**
Herring fishing in the Outer Firth of Forth

**Late September – Christmas**
Herring fishing off the West Coast

**January – February**
Repair of boats and nets, perhaps winter fishing in the Outer Firth of Forth

These seasons corresponded to the different families of herring. The oceanic herring from the Atlantic spawned near the coasts in late winter, spring and summer. It is bigger than herring from the Continental shelf, which spawns at other times of the year, those from the North in later summer and autumn, those from the South near the English east coast in late autumn-December.[20] Thus the herring caught at Shetland would be of the Atlantic kind, whereas the Forth and West Coast herring would be herring of the Northern Continental shelf.

As had been the case with the medieval fisheries in the Sound, where international trade took place alongside the fishing, foreigners came to the Northern Isles to trade. Merchants from Denmark and the Hanseatic towns came to Orkney in July in order to buy fish. Direct trade with Northern Germany is ascertained since about 1410 and for the following three centuries; the traders came from the Hanseatic towns of Hamburg, Bremen, Lübeck, Rostock and Stralsund. In normal years 10 or 12 German merchants traded on Shetland, arriving about 1 June and leaving in August or September. To Shetland they brought fishing equipment and other necessities (hooks, lines, hemp, tar, salt), flour, beer, brandy, tobacco, textiles, shoes, soap and cash, although barter was the usual form of trade. Their return goods were fish and coarse cloth ('vadmel').[21]

In 1491 it was forbidden in Scotland to fish from vessels smaller than 20 tons;[22] in the 16th century the crear was the type of vessel most frequently mentioned. It was a ship of 30-50 tons with a half-deck. By 1600 the East Neuk fishing off the Western and Northern Isles took place from crears; they were used not only for fishing, but also for trade, eg bringing timber from Norway to Scotland.[23]

Scottish fishing is known mainly from statutes, decrees and the like, at least as far as the earlier periods are concerned, and the Exchequer Rolls allow us to gauge its extent. Thus we know that between 1474 and 1599, 61% of the herring exported from the east coast of Scotland had been sent by Anstruther, Crail and Pittenweem, whereas Edinburgh's exports amounted to only 23%.[24] In the 1540s and 1550s the same group of East Neuk towns were the largest exporter of herring from Scotland.[25] But again, these sources allow us to know only the main features of Scottish fishing and not its organization. Who furnished the working capital? Who owned the ships? From where did the salt or the wood for barrels come? To these questions and many more the student of Scottish fishing would like to find an answer.

# The Sources

The student of Southern European economic history will know how much relevant information can be found in the notarial archives, some of which go back to the 12th century. Every kind of contract or obligation would be registered by the notary and has thus in many cases survived until today.

In Northern Europe the institution of the notary or solicitor appeared relatively late; here it was the courts which registered contracts and obligations. From Rostock,[26] Wismar,[27] Stralsund,[28] and Lübeck, the four of them belonging to the Wendic group of the Hanseatic towns, such registers have survived since the 13th century. At Lübeck the registers form two parallel series, the *Oberstadtbuch*,[29] in which transactions concerning real estate were entered, and the *Niederstadtbuch* for other types of obligations; for instance, when a loan had been paid back, the pertaining entry would be crossed out.

In Scotland, this latter type of information can be found in the burgh court books, which have survived for certain towns. At Aberdeen the registers begin in 1398 and continue in an unbroken series (but for a missing volume in the 15th century) until the 19th century; at Dundee and Edinburgh, they begin in the 16th century.

From Crail eight court books have survived in the University Library of St Andrews. They cover the period between October 1552 and February 1591/2, but with gaps. For the last third of the 16th century Protocol Books have survived in the National Archives of Scotland,[30] they contain copies of documents set up by a public notary. Above all they are registers of sasines, but also contain other documents concerning real estate, receipts, obligations as well as marriage contracts and probate records. It is not very likely that they will contain much information on the organization of the fisheries. Like other towns of the region Crail was active in shipping, local as well as long distance.[31]

Fishing held an important place in the town's economic activities, and as it was often financed by loans, these were registered in the burgh court books. In this way, we can follow the individual phases of preparation for the voyage. Obviously, we cannot see all of them for an individual ship, but the number of obligations relating to a particular activity is sufficiently high as to be representative.

As one could expect, the entries were written in different hands and were sometimes crossed out, when the obligation had been paid. However, it is fairly possible that the transactions were entered with a certain delay. On 7 April 1589 William Corstorphine the elder handed over to the bailies on behalf of the town clerk John Makeson a common court book which covered the period from 7 June 1569 to 25 March 1576. As the entry refers to the fee of the scribe,[32] the volume in question must be a fair copy, which was probably based on preliminary notes. The volume can be identified with one of the surviving books, which today contains no entries for the period after 1 March 1574/5. Apparently, the relevant pages have been lost. Other lacunae show that two volumes are missing, one dealing with the period from 1560 to April 1566, the other with the months between April 1584 and February 1588/9. We can thus conclude that the obligations and contracts were not entered immediately after the transaction had taken place; the court books are fair copies which could be written as much as 10 years later.

Between entries dated 22 February 1588/9 and 5 March of the same year the last court book [33] contains a notice by J Orphal, schoolmaster at Kilrenny on the beginning of the year. It is dated 1819; probably then the court books (or at least this volume) were no longer kept in the burgh archives.

Besides the court books of Crail a number of customs books for this period are kept in the National Archives of Scotland. They deal with the harbours of Anstruther, Crail and Pittenweem and do not form a continuous series; they refer to the years 1557, 1566, 1570-1577 and 1582.[34] Their significance resides in the fact that they show us the extent of fishing in the Firth of Forth, which is seldom mentioned in the court books.

Sometimes, the mariners of Crail worked for a merchant in another town, especially Edinburgh (with the Canongate); he would furnish part of the working capital and expect to be paid in fish. The burgh records of Dundee and Edinburgh (with the Canongate) as well as the customs accounts of these towns yield supplementary information on some of these merchants, but generally speaking, our main sources will be the court books of Crail supplemented by the customs records from this town.

# CHAPTER 1

# Getting ready

This chapter deals with the preparations for the voyage as far as barrels, salt and equipment are concerned. The raising of working capital is dealt with in chapter four.

## Barrels

Very often, but not always, the barrel or the last 'Flemish bynd', is mentioned. In all probability, this was an internationally accepted standard measure like the 'Rostocker Band'; in 1375 representatives of the Hanseatic towns in Northern Germany, Prussia, Livonia and on the Zuiderzee had wanted to introduce the barrel of Rostock as the standard measure for herring and beer;[35] it held 830-840 fishes and was accepted as the standard measure for Scanian herring.[36]

At an early date, Scotland similarly recognized the need for standard measures, especially if the cured fish was to be exported. In 1487 Parliament accepted the standard barrel of Hamburg as the official Scottish salmon barrel;[37] later in the year, it was decided that it should hold 14 gallons.[38]Six years later, Parliament voted energetic measures to further Scottish fisheries; in the burghs, fishing ships of at least 20 tuns should be built and the unemployed should be obliged to work on board. Finally, it was decided to recognize the 'auld bind' of Aberdeen as the salmon barrel.[39]

In 1540/1 Parliament decided to introduce standard barrels for salmon, herring and keiling (cod) throughout Scotland, but they were not described.[40] In January 1570/1 the Convention of Royal Burghs had defined the herring barrel as 10 gallons,[41] but in 1573 Parliament defined standard barrels for all Scotland; the salmon barrel should hold 12 gallons of the Stirling pint, and the barrel for herring or white fish nine gallons.[42] Nine gallons herring would thus correspond to *c* 1.22 hl. (hectolitres).[43]

In 1581, the Convention of Royal Burghs underlined that according to an Act of Parliament (apparently not to be found in the printed edition) the Scottish herring barrel should be of the Flemish bind, which was confirmed in 1584.[44] Thus at least from 1573 the measure held *c* 1.22 hl. The history of prices for Flanders and Brabant gives only the herring barrel of Antwerp, which held *c* 800 salted fishes.[45]

Besides the Flemish barrel, which dominated the herring fishing, we find a smaller barrel 'of ye small bind'[46] as well as the puncheon of two barrels.[47] Sometimes the barrels are counted individually, sometimes in lasts of 12 barrels.

Frequently, the contracts oblige the furnisher of barrels, often a cooper, to deliver a specific quantity of barrels at a later date, and we may infer that often the person who placed the order had paid in advance, thus giving the furnisher working capital.[48]

In rare cases the commissioner would furnish the necessary wood instead of money. Thus on 12 April 1580, William Smyth, cooper, obliged himself to deliver to William Morton by Christmas 1580 two Flemish barrels of herring from Northern Scotland plus ten lasts of Flemish barrels, which he should produce at his own cost. In return William Morton obliged himself to put the necessary wood at Smyth's disposal.[49]

The time agreed for the production of barrels varied a great deal. Often the date of delivery would be a date in late summer, when the fishing season approached, mainly at Lammas (1 August) or Little St Mary's (8 September), but Easter, Whitsuntide or Christmas were also mentioned. Generally the time of production was calculated as about four months, but also very short times were sometimes specified. In these cases, a previous time had been exceeded, or the production of barrels was part of the payment of an overdue debt.[50] The cooper David Currour was late in delivering his barrels more than once; besides the case just mentioned, in February 1556/7 the court, acting on John Symson's behalf, obliged him to produce the barrels within one and two weeks respectively. In the latter case (delivery of 32 lasts of barrels within two weeks), he was to pay a fine of three shillings if he failed.[51]

In several examples failure to deliver within the agreed time would oblige the cooper to pay to his creditor an amount corresponding to the highest market price.[52] The same rule applied to the fisherman, if he did not deliver his fish in time. It served a double purpose: it allowed the creditor to buy his barrels or fish elsewhere without loss, and it obliged the cooper or the fisherman to finish his work in time. As the fishing season approached, the demand for barrels would increase, with rising prices as a consequence. Any delay would thus cause a loss to the cooper. Unfortunately, only in some years is the price of the barrel mentioned. In Table 2, the lowest, the highest and the average prices are given, as well as the number of cases.

Sometimes, the coopers would buy their wood from a merchant, mainly at Crail itself.[53] Also, the coopers of Crail would generally work within the local market at Crail; as far as barrels and wood were concerned, economic relations with the outside world were rare. There were two cases with Dundonians,[54] one with Anstruther,[55] one with Pittenweem,[56] and perhaps one with a merchant of the Canongate, [57] that is all.

It was a problem to find convenient timber in Scotland. There were indeed native forests, but situated in regions of difficult access and, (unlike Norway and Sweden), Scottish rivers were little suited for floating.

Consequently, wood had to be imported, mainly from Norway. Here the cutting of the logs into deals took place when the rivers had abundant water in autumn or in spring. The Scots arrived in great numbers, in small vessels, and bought their timber directly from the producers, who were generally peasants, and often freeholders. The Scots could furnish corn in return, which as a rule the Norwegians had to import.[58]

The court books reveal that some of the coopers of Crail organized voyages to Norway for this purpose, eg John Anderson, who in 1567 could have sailed to Norway himself; on 18 November, he claimed against William Kay 'for ye baringe' (freight) of 30,000 'heringe pryfe' (quality control) (4d. the thousand or altogether 10s.).[59]

In May 1568, John Morton, cooper, recognized his debt of £15 to his partner in a voyage (destination not mentioned), which should be paid by 15 August.[60] In the following year, skipper Thomas Davidson claimed £14 from John Morton for his part of the charter of Thomas Davidson's ship for a voyage to Norway.[61] Again in 1572, John Morton went to Norway.[62]

The best documented voyages, however, were those of 1571. In April, John Morton chartered the *Marie Anne*, which belonged to George Peirson and Andrew Balcony, for two voyages to Norway.[63] At the same time, Morton received from Mr Thomas Ramsay two obligations to a value of £105, moreover Morton acknowledged a debt of £50 to John Melville. Morton obliged himself to pay Melville 20 merks (or £13-4) on his return from his first voyage and the same amount on his second return; by 24 August he should deliver to Melville two lasts of Flemish barrels as well as 11 puncheons and by 8 September pay the remaining sum of £23-6-8. [64] As Morton charged 20 merks for each voyage, and as Melville was to furnish a quarter of the cargo,[65] we can infer that Morton paid the 20 merks due on his return from each voyage, through his services.

As we learn from Morton's settlement with skipper Thomas Davidson,[66] the latter was to be the master of the ship. Furthermore he procured half the cargo on behalf of Morton. After the first voyage

Morton set out again for Norway, but must have returned by 25 July when he promised Thomas Davidson 7 ½ lasts of Flemish barrels as payment for his remaining debt of £12. On the last day of August, Davidson gave Morton the general discharge for their partnership.[67]

Thus Morton provided half the cargo, John Melville one quarter,[68] but the sources are silent about the last quarter. It could have belonged to James Clark of Burntisland; on 25 April Patrick Lindsay and William Arnot stood surety for his debt of £28-10 to one of the *Marie Anne*'s owners, to be paid by 24 June, thus after her return from Norway.[69] However, this is only one among several possibilities.

Morton must have used another ship for his second voyage to Norway as he recognised his debt of £6-11 for the remaining 'feand', (charter of a ship), to William Arnot.[70] Not all the wood brought back from Norway was for Morton's own use; he also provided wood for other coopers. Thus in November David Currour acknowledged owing Morton money for 143 'knappit', ie knapholt or clapboard.[71] Nor was it the first time that John Melville had engaged in the Norway trade. In April 1571, he still owed £25 to the owners of the *Marie Anne* for freight, which because of the date probably refers to a voyage in 1570.[72] Moreover, on 4 December 1571, John Morton acknowledged his debt of £80 to John Melville to be paid in equal instalments of £40 by 8 September 1572 and by the same date in 1573. Probably this sum was intended as part of Morton's working capital for further voyages to be undertaken in 1572 and 1573. As already mentioned, Morton did go to Norway in 1572, but on the voyage planned for 1573 the sources are silent.

It is probable that most coopers of Crail bought their wood locally, only John Morton engaged himself in the timber trade with Norway, and as we have seen, he went abroad himself in order to choose the kind of wood to buy and to negotiate with the Norwegian timber merchants. With working capital furnished by his partners he chartered a ship, engaged a skipper and furnished part of the cargo. The wood and timber brought to Crail from Norway he partly used himself and sold the rest to others. We do not know whether or not other coopers worked for him in a putting out system, here again the sources are silent.

About 20 years later, we have got another example of coopers, who took part in the timber trade with Norway. The skipper John Martin and the coopers John Myrton and James Lauder formed a partnership for a voyage to Norway; on 11 April 1590, they obliged themselves to deliver to William Hunter 100 deals, 18 or at least 16 feet long and one foot broad. Hunter had already paid them, and they were to give him half the timber on their return and the rest by 1 August, or to pay the equivalent of the highest market price.[73]

Also the partners obliged themselves to furnish Alan Cunningham with 50 deals of the same kind by 1 August: by the same date, the coopers were to deliver to him five lasts of Flemish barrels.[74] Moreover, John Myrton promised to deliver to John Parkie three lasts of Flemish barrels by 8 September.[75]

This case of 1590 can be compared with those of 1571. The coopers formed a partnership with the skipper and they went to Norway themselves in order to buy the timber. Before their departure they had got orders, which were paid in advance, and in this way the partners obtained part of their working capital. What matters in these examples is the fact that the coopers did not rely on the expert knowledge of others, but went to Norway in person.[76]

In the 1640s Scottish skippers often engaged in a triangular trade between Scotland, the Low Countries and Norway: Scottish goods were sold in the Low Countries, where other goods were acquired. In Norway part of the cargo was sold, timber was bought and taken to Scotland.[77] Unfortunately, our sources do not allow us to ascertain whether or not a similar trade took place in the second half of the 16th century.

## Salt

In order to cure herring, salt is necessary. The best and most expensive quality was that of Lüneburg in Northern Germany, which was preferred for the cure of Scanian herring. In the 15th century, salt from Western France became a serious rival, at least in the Baltic herring fisheries. In England and Scotland salt was produced from the sea, and much of the salt needed for the local fishery was probably produced in Scotland: the latter was called 'small salt' while foreign salt was called 'great salt'.[78]

Four entries in the court books refer to the trade in salt. The first case involved William Annand and John Ryd, concerning 18 bolls of salt at the price of 24s. each. The court found that William Annand and John Digvaill should receive the salt from John Ryd, when they returned from Loch Broom.[79]

William Annand was also involved in the second transaction. On 27 August 1578, David Currour, cooper, obliged himself to deliver to William Annand two lasts of Flemish barrels within two weeks. Moreover, Annand had sold him 20 barrels of small salt for £15 to be paid by Martinmas (11 November). If Currour failed to do so, by Christmas he was to deliver five lasts of Flemish barrels to Annand. Finally, Currour by Martinmas 1578 was to furnish to Annand five dozen fir deals ('fyrue dailes').[80] Like other coopers, Currour traded in timber as well; whether Annand regularly traded in salt or not cannot be ascertained: apparently, he was a general merchant.[81]

Thirdly, on 7 May 1590 Andro Davidson the elder recognised his debt of £48-10 to Duncan Balfour of St Andrews to be paid by 8 September. For this sum Thomas Beane, mariner, and William Hunter stood security, and in return, Davidson put his crear, the *Marie Rose*, at their disposal. From another entry of the same date we learn that Davidson prepared a voyage to the Northern Isles, as he promised to pay his debt to Balfour in fish.[82]

Thomas Beane also planned a voyage. On 18 May 1590, he borrowed from James Wade in Lambieletham £34-13-4 and from David Alexander of Crail £45, both sums to be paid by 8 September.[83] Beane bought four chalders of salt for £42 (to be paid by 1 July) from Mr Andrew Sandilandis.[84] Beane's declaration of 16 June shows us that the purpose of the voyage (destination Shetland) was trade and not fishing. He formed a partnership with William Hunter, using the *Marie Rose*, which belonged to Andro Davidson the elder. Part of the cargo consisted of salt: 30 bolls grit salt and five chalders small salt; five eighths of the salt belonged to Beane. Apparently, Beane had borrowed £15 to buy the small salt and paid to William 'Boill' (?) freight £3 for the grit salt and £3-10 for the small salt.

The *Marie Rose* carried goods belonging to more partnerships. Again with William Hunter, Beane ventured one puncheon of claret[85] and with John Corstorphine three puncheons of English 'beir' (beer) to Shetland. William 'Boill' (to whom Beane paid the freight of the salt), must have been the master of the vessel. According to Beane's declaration of 16 June, the *Marie Rose* had not yet returned. Beane was preparing yet another voyage and could for this reason not be at Crail in order to receive his part of the profit on the sale of salt, wine, and beer. Consequently, he authorized his father-in-law David Alexander, and George Beane, to receive it on his behalf.[86] In all likelihood, he had organised the voyage, but did not sail to Shetland himself.

## Nets, lines and other equipment

For a voyage of several weeks to the fishing grounds off Northern Scotland, Shetland, or the Western Isles, the ship would need provisions and nautical instruments. As these items are never mentioned in the court books, we do not know who should procure them. Unlike today, the master was not bound to an individual ship; thus it is possible that the nautical instruments belonged to him and not to the owners of the vessel. Whether the master, the charterers or the individual members of the crew procured the provisions, we do not know. On the other hand, when the court obliged Thomas Robertson to serve mariner Robert Burne for a year, the latter was to give him, inter alia, two pairs of shoes and other pieces of clothing, as well as 12 hooks for a great line and 50 for small lines.[87]

Besides barrels, (already discussed), nets and lines were necessary. Nets were used in the herring fisheries, but the other important catch, keiling, was taken on lines. As his inheritance from the late Thomas Wemyss, the sailor ('seman') James Corstorphine was to receive from Thomas Kay and Agnes Kay (widow of Thomas Wemyss), one Shetland herring net with four 'bowes' and 'ye bow towis' (= buoy ropes, ie the ropes between the boat and the buoy, from which the lines or nets were suspended), seven keiling hand lines, eight 'laidstones' (ie leaden sinkers for fishing handlines) and one dozen keiling hand line hooks.[88]

Herring and keiling were caught at the same time, as we learn from William Davidson's contract with John Bruce to whom he owed £4. In return Davidson obliged himself to engage one of Bruce's men for the next fisheries off Shetland; Bruce was to equip him with a herring net, one great line and a half, two keiling hand lines and two laidstones. At the end of the venture, Davidson was to give the gear back to Bruce along with his servant's share of the fish. As a member of the crew, Bruce's servant must have been entitled to part of the catch. [89]

As to the value of the equipment, our information is scanty: in 1559 a herring net was estimated at 40d.[90] The significance of the equipment is underlined in a contract of apprenticeship as a fisherman. For 12 years from Whitsuntide 1553 William Walker engaged as an apprentice with John Galloway and his wife.[91] If he chose to remain in their service for a thirteenth year, the couple were to give him three herring nets, one 'grethyng' (great line, ie a long line used in deep sea fishing for eg cod or ling) and one 'smallyng of xx scor' (small line, ie a line used by inshore fishermen for catching smaller fish).[92]

CHAPTER 2

# The fishing grounds
# and their seasons

This chapter deals with the individual fishing regions and the time of the year when they were visited. Obviously, as the court books register loans and other obligations, destinations far away tend to be over represented, as these ventures needed more capital. Consequently, the near fisheries like those off the east coast of Scotland and in the Firth of Forth will be under represented in the court books. Nevertheless, fishing in the Firth of Forth was important, as the surviving customs records tell us.

## The Northern Isles: Orkney and Shetland

As destinations the court books mention Orkney, Shetland and the Northern Isles. Although both groups of islands belong to the Northern Isles, for methodological reasons each destination is considered separately.

Orkney is mentioned only once. In 1569, skipper of Crail John Davidson let to William Lyall and John Paterson, both of Pittenweem, for £20, his boat the *Martin* with full equipment for a voyage to Orkney or Shetland. They were to load their cargo in Orkney or Shetland and to unload it at Crail, Pittenweem or any other convenient port. No date by which the debt should be paid is given, nor is an equivalent in fish mentioned.[93] As other entries of the same month refer to fishing voyages to Loch Carron or to Northern Scotland, the scope of Lyall's and Paterson's venture was probably trade rather than fishing. This is confirmed by the fact that the main fishing off Shetland took place between April and September according to the kind of fish sought; thus the open boats catching herring were active from June to August and the half-decked crears from late August to late September. The latter were frequently used also in East Neuk fishing off the Western Isles. Moreover, dry fish (cod and ling) was loaded in Shetland from the end of July until the middle of October and herring from the middle of July until the end of February.[94] Consequently, Lyall and Paterson could simply have been carriers of fish.

One other voyage, this time to Shetland, can be explained in the same way,[95] but otherwise most entries refer to actual fishing off Shetland. The fishing in late spring and in early summer is shown by several entries: on 29 June 1568 the court obliged Henry Lou to give security to James Scrymgeour when he came back from Shetland,[96] and on 4 May 1576 William Davidson promised to engage one of John Bruce's servants for his voyage to Shetland in the next season of fishing.[97]

The ling fishing off Shetland began about 1 June and continued until about 1 September.[98] The venture of Steven Arnot of Crail and George Bell of Fisherrow confirms these dates. On 29 April 1583 they obliged themselves to deliver to George Corstorphine of Crail 1,000 'fres leinges' caught off Shetland; they were to receive the agreed working capital by 15 August. If they caught no fish, the working capital was to be paid back to Corstorphine.[99] An entry a few days later gives us further particulars. Bell appears to have furnished the ship and her crew, and with Arnot he obliged himself to deliver 1,500 keiling to John Hamilton of Edinburgh. Apparently, the crew also got a certain share of the profit.[100]

Winter fishing must also have taken place off Shetland. On 16 September 1579 William Arnot acknowledged a debt of £20 to Margaret Gowan in return for which he promised to deliver to her by 1 January 1579/80 one last herring Flemish bind caught off Shetland or to pay her the equivalent of the highest market price. Further, he obliged himself to give her eight barrels of herring by Christmas 1579.[101]

Another example of a late Shetland venture, probably for fishing, was that of Duncan Laury and David Mackie. On 18 November 1567, they agreed each to pay half their rent of Andrew Morris's equipment, ie a 'cadoraun' (cauldron) and 'broum loumis' (brewing lume, ie a vat for brewing) for a Shetland voyage within the year, ie before 24 March 1567/8. [102]

Apparently then, the main Shetland fishing took place in late spring and during the summer with a smaller season in winter. For the fishermen of Crail there were two main seasons, whose dates the source does not specify: 'ye owtreik to ye Zetland fisheis and…ye owtreik to ye North Isles'.[103]

One entry refers to a dispute between Alexander Inglis and John Mercer. The latter had borrowed £10 from Inglis and claimed to have delivered to him on various occasions three half-barrels of Northern Isles herring according to the price. In December 1586, 1587 and 1588 it was £3-3-4 for half a barrel, thus a total of £9-10.[104] As we shall see, the contracts between the mariners and fishermen on one side and their furnishers of working capital on the other were made in September with payment in fish by Christmas. Thus it was only logical that the December prices were mentioned. The case allows us to assume that autumn fishing took place off the Northern Isles in the years 1586-8.

From September 1590 a considerable number of entries have survived (Tables 20-21), which all deal with obligations of mariners or fishermen towards the lenders of working capital; the amount was to be paid back by Christmas in herring caught off the Northern Isles. Frequently the contracts mention the possibility that the fishermen could catch only part of the promised fish. If two thirds could be had, they were to deliver two thirds of the agreed quantity and to pay the last third in cash. Generally, the value of a last of Northern Isles herring was estimated at £44. If Andrew Davidson could get no fish at all, he was to pay the equivalent of the highest market price of the promised last of herring plus £20, which he had received with the estimated equivalent of one last of herring, £40. This would mean that he would be obliged to pay £64 (the reimbursement of the received £60 plus an indemnity of £4).[105]

As Orkney and Shetland belong to the Northern Isles, the destination Northern Isles could refer to both groups of islands. However, frequently, the burgh court books confusingly use the term of the Northern Isles for the Hebrides. Probably, the mariners could not know in advance, where they could find the herring. Further, it would be fair to mention only the general region; if the mariner had obliged himself to furnish Shetland herring and could find the shoal only off Orkney, could one then argue that he did not respect his contract ?

Although late spring and early summer were the main period of fishing off Shetland, some fishing took place in autumn as well. In the autumn of 1590 however, there were comprehensive fisheries off the Northern Isles, which could mean that the herring shoals began to turn up in autumn there also.

## Loch Broom

This fishing ground is situated off present-day Ullapool. By 1566, its fishing had been recognized internationally as advantageous as foreigners asked for permission to fish there. The Scottish government convoked experienced burgesses to a meeting with the Privy Council. Having heard their opinion, it decided to reserve the fishing in Loch Broom and other lochs for Scottish nationals.[106] Both Dundee and Aberdeen participated in the trade that arose from the fishing at Loch Broom; in December 1566, Dundee received 153 barrels of Loch Broom herring and in 1576, 348 barrels; in 1583, at least 175 barrels of Loch Broom herring were exported from Aberdeen. Moreover, in 1587, many vessels called at Aberdeen on their way back from Loch Broom.[107] In the 1570s, a great part of the herring export from the Crail group came from the Western Highlands, ie Loch Broom, Loch Carron and related places.[108]

The fishermen of Crail visited it mainly in the 1560s. The obligations were registered in September and the term of delivery was 2 February[109] or on return (Tables 20-21).[110]

It is not mentioned whether or not the fishermen were allowed to furnish other kinds of fish like keiling, if herring was not to be had in sufficient quantities. In 1568, David Hawson and Alexander Bikarton promised to pay to their furnisher of capital, John Dingwall, 'profeit for his mony as cumes to five pound ye scur' (25 %), if no herring could be taken.[111] The term of reckoning in February appears to be confirmed by two cases from 1566/7. On 4 February, the court obliged Andrew Peirson and William Gilruth ('Gilrouiht') to pay within a week £30 'lyuht mony' (light money, ie under the standard or legal weight) to William Buffy 'to pas to Loucht Browm',[112] and one week later William Birnie of Edinburgh sued William Kay for two lasts of Loch Broom herring or the equivalent of the highest price in cash.[113]

Sometimes the reckoning was delayed, as we saw in William Buffy's case; in May 1567 Janet Symson, Thomas Grot's widow, acknowledged a debt of £4 to Andrew Martyn as the last instalment of £25 'of Loucht Brown vaigis', ie for a voyage to Loch Broom; £2 should be paid by Martinmas 1567 and the rest by 2 February 1567/8. As the initial obligation was dated 24 September 1566, the voyage must have taken place in the autumn of 1566.[114] Not only fishermen or mariners participated in the voyages to Loch Broom; thus in November 1567 Robert Mur, cooper, was obliged to pay a debt when he returned.[115]

If in the 1560s the Loch Broom fishing took place in autumn, one case from 1578 indicates an earlier date in the season. In this year, Andrew Melville of Anstruther had furnished to John Melville of Crail one last and two barrels herring caught in Loch Broom at a price of £37 the last or a total of £43-3-4. Of this, £9 had been paid at the delivery of the fish; the remaining sum should be paid by Christmas 1578.[116] Had the Loch Broom season moved to spring? Not definitely, because 11 years later a number of loans were registered on 29 July at the Burgh Court of St Andrews, referring to the fisheries in Loch Broom.[117]

In 1586 the Convention of Royal Burghs complained to the Privy Council that their fishing off Northern Scotland and the Isles was being disturbed by a number of named Highlanders.[118] According to the Burghs the fishing was free, but under James V and Mary of Guise's regency the rule had been introduced that for each last of fish caught at the Isles the fishermen should pay 3s.4d. to the owner of the ground, for ground leave (use of the land, in this case the shore must be meant), anchorage etc. On top of that customs should be paid in one of the free (ie royal) burghs.

The afore-mentioned Highlanders had claimed supplementary duties from the fishermen; when for instance the fishermen had constructed sheds with their own timber, which they would cover with the sails of their ship, they were charged £8 for the shed. As none of the convoked Highlanders appeared before the Privy Council, this body put them to the horn as rebels. On the same day, it forbade the exportation of fish, especially Loch Broom herring, until the Scottish market had been provided for.[119]

The trade in herring from the Western Highlands flourished in the 1560s and declined in the 1580s and 1590s, perhaps because of unrest in the Isles.[120] In 1576 Rory Macleod of Lewis and his son Torquil promised the Privy Council not to disturb legal Scottish fishing in 'the

Lochis of the Lewis, or in utheris the North Ylis of this realme.'[121] Three years later John, Bishop of the Isles, complained to the Privy Council of various members of the Clan Maclean and others who prevented him and his servants from visiting the diocese, as well as merchants, mariners and fishermen from the pursuit of their trade.[122]

These examples as well as the one already mentioned from 1586 tell us that fishing was hindered by unrest in the Isles, but in some years herring was rare. For this reason the Privy Council forbade the export of herring because of its scarcity in Loch Broom and other northern places on 30 November 1586 as well as on 27 January 1587/8.[123] Again in the autumn of 1590 fishing must have been unsatisfactory. Because of the scarcity of fish and consequently high prices, the Privy Council allowed people to eat meat in periods of Lent.[124]

Loch Broom was visited not only by fishermen of Crail in the 1560s, in 1578 and in 1589, but regularly by those of other towns like Dundee. It is thus possible that some of the ships of Crail mentioned in the sources as bound for Northern Scotland could have caught their fish in Loch Broom. Among the fishing grounds in the Minch, Loch Broom was particularly important because of the abundance of herring appearing year after year.[125] The fishing was in the hands of mariners and fishermen from the Lowlands and had consequently only marginal significance for the economy of the Western Isles or even for the diet of their inhabitants.[126] As a rule, boats and their equipment belonged to the inhabitants of the Scottish east coast, and if they engaged local people (mainly cottars or fishermen), it was only as workers.[127]

## Loch Carron

By this designation is meant the innermost part of a firth on the east side of the Inner Sound between the Isle of Skye and the mainland. In 1569, the only year of the period that it is possible to investigate, a number of fishermen of Crail went there for herring. It must mean, however, that when the contracts were made, the prospect of fishing was promising; unfortunately we do not know why. Had the fishing in Loch Carron been good in 1568? Our sources are silent. In most cases 'Northern Scotland' is mentioned as a subsidiary destination; if no fish were to be had in Loch Carron, the fishermen were free to try their luck elsewhere off Northern Scotland.

Most contracts were registered in September, but the term of delivery was seldom mentioned (Tables 20-21). In two cases, 2 February 1569/70 was specified, and on one occasion the English furnisher of capital, Robert Constable of Wellington, wanted to receive his fish at Newcastle by Shrove Tuesday, ie 7 February 1569/70. If other terms were mentioned, it would be at their return, within a week, or within 48 hours, after their arrival at Crail.

If herring was not to be had in sufficient quantities, the fishermen were often allowed to deliver keiling instead. If neither was to be had, the sum advanced had to be paid back.[128] One contract stipulates that if eight or only four lasts of herring were caught, Alexander Farmer was obliged to deliver to his creditors half a last (otherwise he should furnish them one last) and pay them half the advanced amount; if no fish were found, the whole sum was to be reimbursed.[129] In another case, Andro Corstorphine obliged himself to deliver at Leith half a last of herring or keiling.[130] As, at this time, Leith was one of the most important ports for trade with the Continent,[131] the herring was probably intended for export. This is confirmed by the clause that if the skipper was to sail to Bordeaux or westwards (to Ireland ?), Corstorphine should keep the fish on board, sell it and make the reckoning on his return.[132] The dates of the entries show us that the fishing took place in the autumn, which is confirmed by a case of spoliation in Loch Carron of a ship belonging to the Englishman Walter Dawlis in October 1569; i.a. 31 dozen 'satte' (ie coalfish) were taken by the Scots. The owner of the offending Scottish vessel was John Davidson of Crail, her skipper was James Davidson.[133]

Voyages to Loch Broom and Loch Carron are only specifically mentioned in the late 1560s. Later the destinations were often given

as Northern Scotland; probably the fishermen and mariners kept all
their options open, as they realised that the herring could suddenly
disappear from a place where it had been abundant.

## The Isles

According to the burgh court books of Crail, fishing off 'the Isles'
took place only between 1577 and 1584, especially in 1581 and 1582
[134] (Tables 20-21). Several times it is specified that herring from 'the
Isles' came from 'Northern Scotland'. [135] In general, delivery was to
take place at Christmas (when a day was mentioned); in two cases
other dates are given; the end of November[136] and 1 January.[137] Thus
fishing at 'the Isles' took place in autumn, which makes it less probable
that the Northern Isles (Orkney, Shetland) were meant. In all likelihood then 'the Isles' should be identified with the Western Isles or
the Hebrides, but the sources allow no further specification. Whereas
the obligations referring to Loch Broom or Loch Carron were mainly
registered in September, those dealing with fishing at 'the Isles' were
often registered in spring.

Many obligations contain the usual clause that if no fish were
delivered by the agreed date, the lender should receive the equivalent
of the highest market price. Nevertheless, in spite of the fact that John
Melville the younger had not delivered the promised last of herring
to Andrew Melville the younger of Anstruther in time, the amount
owed (£40) does not appear to be higher than the usual estimate of a
last of herring.[138]

On 11 March 1577/8 Robert and Peter Arnot acknowledged their
debt of £44 to Mr John Harte of the Canongate as the price of one
last Isles herring. On 7 September 1576 they had received from John
Harte £60 with the obligation to deliver to him by Christmas 1576
two lasts of herring from Northern Scotland, but had given him only
one last.[139] When in September 1576 the contract had been set up,
a last of herring was reckoned at £30; the price of £44 thus reflected

the highest market price. That this was reasonable, is confirmed by John Dawson's obligation from 4 October 1577, which estimated a last at £45.

A similar case was registered in March 1584. John Mertene acknowledged a debt of £50 to John Summerville of Edinburgh. Mertene and Edward Spens had obliged themselves to deliver a last of Isles herring to Summerville and apparently failed to do so. Consequently the price was fixed at £50, which must have corresponded to the highest market price.[140]

Also another merchant of Edinburgh, John Galloway, engaged himself in the fishing at the Isles. At any rate, 10 lasts and a half of Isles herring belonged to him and made up part of the cargo of the *Thomas*, whose owner was Thomas Martin of Crail,[141] probably the same man who had participated in the fishing in Loch Carron in 1569.

## Northern Scotland

We saw already that the fishing grounds in Loch Broom, in Loch Carron and off the Western Isles could be considered as parts of 'Northern Scotland'. When the latter destination was given, the skipper probably wanted to keep all possibilities open and, if necessary, to try his luck at other places in the region as initially planned. No records have survived for 1575 and for 1584-8, and after the year of the Spanish Armada only one obligation was registered in 1589. In 1578-9 few entries were made, at least in comparison with the other years between 1569 and 1583. As all the obligations of 1569 refer to Loch Carron or 'Northern Scotland', the destination of the voyage has been considered as Loch Carron.

Many contracts mention that if no herring was to be had, keiling could be taken in its place. In general, no specification is given, but George Corstorphine, who was to deliver nine barrels of herring to James Monipenny, obliged himself to give him five barrels of herring and four of keiling, if little herring could be caught.[142] Another contract contains the curious clause that two fishermen obliged themselves to deliver, if they caught one last of herring, just half a last, but if they caught two lasts, then they would deliver one last.[143] Moreover, several contracts contain a clause of indemnity, eg on 4 September 1570, John Dowekand sold to William Annand one last of herring Flemish bind from 'Northern Scotland' at a price of £26, which he had received. The fish were to be delivered by Christmas 1570; keiling could be substituted, if no herring could be caught. If neither kind of fish was to be had, Dowekand should pay Annand £30, ie the received estimated price of £26 with an indemnity of £4. If in due course Dowekand was able to furnish a last of herring, but from another region than 'Northern Scotland', the price should be reduced by 21s.[144]

Sometimes the contract left room for improvisation. John Smith acknowledged his debt of £11 to Patrick Geddes which should be paid by Christmas 1572. If however the *Mary James*, in which Smith owned a part, would leave for 'Northern Scotland', probably for fishing, the term of payment could be delayed until Easter 1573.[145] Moreover, George Peirson obliged himself to give to Patrick Lindsay the fourth part of his cargo, 'off quhatsumeuer guids gair qlk he sal happen to gett in the northern partis off this realme.' The date of the entry makes it probable that a fishing venture was meant.[146] Another contract registered two days earlier obliged William Gilbert and John Greif to furnish to David Beane herring and whiting, but if no herring could be had, keiling could be taken in its place.[147]

On 2 September 1573, Alexander Farmer acknowledged his debt of £58 to John Malwyll, obliging himself to deliver two lasts of herring at Crail. If no herring was caught, he was to pay the sum back within two weeks of his return. Moreover, the contract contained the clause that 18 barrels should be taken from William Annand's crear and six barrels from the one governed by Andro Baxter. If the two vessels got only the quarter of a full cargo, Farmer should furnish only one last of herring.[148] The case shows us that Farmer was not the master of the ships, but that he was responsible for the fishing, further that Malwyll divided his support and consequently also his risk between the two crears.

Farmer's role as an organizer of the fishing is confirmed by another case from the same year. Thomas Moreis obliged himself to deliver to Alexander Farmer half a last of herring by Christmas 1573, if he should catch at least one last.[149] An enigmatic contract can probably be explained in a similar way. Nicol John acknowledged a debt of £24 to Patrick Lindsay, and David Scott was to deliver a barrel of herring by Christmas 1573.[150] Here Nicol John appears to have been the organizer with Scott as the mariner.

Sometimes the choice of the port of landing was left to the discretion of the master. Thus, John 'Caddowy' of Anstruther obliged himself to deliver a last of herring at Crail, Pittenweem, Anstruther, St Andrews, Dundee or any port at which he would call by Christmas 1576.[151]

One furnisher of capital, Patrick Hogg of Kirkcaldy, left the possibility open that the herring could be abundant; in this case the mariners obliged themselves to furnish him more fish than foreseen in the contract. If George Peirson got 15 lasts of herring in his crear (possibly the maximum cargo ?) or only half cargo, he was to furnish him with three lasts of herring instead of the two otherwise stipulated, and John Martyne and his partners agreed to give Hogg 18 barrels of herring more than the three lasts mentioned in the contract, if they caught nine or even only six lasts in their crear.[152]

## Other destinations

A few entries refer to other destinations than those already mentioned. We learn that John Gray accompanied his master Thomas Davidson to the fishing off Peterhead,[153] and in 1576 David Scott of Crail obliged himself to deliver to James Meldrum of Crail two lasts of herring Flemish bind from 'ye eist landis' at £30 the last. As payment Scott had already received 24 bolls of 'gryt salt' at 47s. Scots each, or £56-8.

The herring was to be delivered at Crail, Dundee or Pittenweem. If Scott could get only half a cargo, he was to give Meldrum one last and pay the rest; if he got no herring at all, he should pay Meldrum £76 at Christmas, thus with an indemnity of £16.[154] What in this context 'ye eist landis' means, is difficult to ascertain; usually, the expression would denote the Baltic region, but it could also refer to the fisheries in the Danish Limfjord or off Marstrand in the Norwegian-Swedish frontier region.

Only three entries mention herring fishing in the Firth of Forth, but because of its vicinity to Crail the ships would not be absent for long and written contracts would not always be necessary. In December 1576 Steven Arnot promised to deliver one last of Forth herring to Walter Ballingall by 2 February 1576/7 or to pay the equivalent of the highest market price.[155] Also Robert Arnot obliged himself to catch a last of herring Flemish bind in the Firth of Forth and deliver it to John Harte of Canongate by 15 August or to pay him the equivalent of the highest market price.[156] Further, in February 1582/3 Arthur Gray of Crail obliged himself to deliver to Steven Balfour of St Andrews 18 barrels herring Flemish bind caught "within yis fyrthe and reuer of Forthe" by 8 September at Crail. If no herring could be had, Gray should pay back £48 which he had already received. If there was herring and Gray did not deliver it, he should pay Balfour £57, ie the received amount plus a compensation of £9.[157] About a month later Gray sold one half of the crear the *Harry* to Ninian Woide for £100, but the transaction could be revoked, if by 8 September Gray paid the £100.[158] In this way Gray procured himself working capital for the fishing season in the Forth, which must have been in the late spring or in summer.

Thus it is clear that the main fishing grounds at any distance were to be found in Northern Scotland, on its west coast in the late 1560s, off the Western Isles between 1577 and 1584 and off Shetland. Nevertheless, the customs accounts show us that the fisheries in the Firth of Forth played a greater role than revealed by the entries in the burgh court books.

## The fishing seasons

In the great majority of cases the contracts were registered in September, and Christmas was agreed upon as the date by which the fish should be delivered. So it was for the vessels fishing off Northern Scotland in the 1570s and 1580s and off the Northern Isles in 1590. It appears safe to reckon that three months was the average duration of the voyage to and from the destinations, where the fishing took place in autumn.

The contracts which refer to Loch Broom and Loch Carron reveal a slightly different chronology. Here too the majority of contracts were made in September, but the main dates of delivery were fixed in February or at return of the vessel. This could indicate longer times for voyages than those to the Northern Isles or to Northern Scotland. As far as the Hebrides were concerned contracts were registered from February to October with a concentration in March and April. As a rule the date of delivery was at the end of the year with a concentration at Christmas. Obviously, the voyage from Crail was longer than that to the other fishing grounds, but this circumstance is probably not sufficient to explain the number of months between the contract and the delivery of the fish. Probably, then, the herring appeared earlier at the Western Isles than off Northern Scotland or the Northern Isles. As fishing in Loch Broom and Loch Carron is documented during the 1570s and 1580s,[159] we can assume that many of the voyages to Northern Scotland registered at Crail actually went to Loch Broom or Loch Carron.

Perhaps we can reconstruct the seasonal pattern of appearance of the herring shoals as follows.

Western shoals: Hebrides in summer, Northern Scotland autumn, Northern Isles autumn, from there to the south along the east coast of Scotland and England.

Northern shoals: Northern Isles late spring and summer, from there to the south along the east coast of Scotland and England.

Obviously, this seasonal pattern of appearance must to a large extent remain hypothetical, as only further research can furnish more solid details.

# CHAPTER 3

# The catch and the quantities

## The catch

Herring was by far the most important fish caught by the vessels of Crail, but frequently we find the clause that if no herring was to be had, keiling (cod) could be delivered in its stead. This stipulation we find above all in contracts registered 1569-72.[160] In a few cases keiling was considered less valuable than herring. In 1569 Andro Bikarton, Thomas Mertyne and George Corstorphine obliged themselves to deliver to William Annand three lasts and a half of Loch Carron herring in return for £84 received; on top of that they should give him 14 barrels of herring. If no herring was to be had, they could deliver seven lasts of keiling in its stead; if neither kind of fish was caught, the money had to be paid back. If the 14 barrels were to be considered as interest, this would correspond to four barrels per last of herring or to 33%.[161]

In September 1571 George Corstorphine obliged himself to deliver to James Monipenny nine barrels of herring from Northern Scotland; Monipenny had advanced £20 to him. If herring could not be caught in sufficient quantities, Corstorphine was to deliver five barrels of herring and four of keiling.[162]

The last example was registered in November 1581. Arthur Gray and John Paterson of Crail promised to deliver to John Harte of the Canongate two lasts of herring from Northern Scotland by 1 March 1581/2. If no herring was to be had, Hacke would accept 26 barrels of keiling in its stead. In this case the two supplementary barrels of keiling must be considered an indemnity of 8 1/3%. If neither fish was to be found, the £60 received should be paid back to Harte.[163]

We have seen that keiling could be substituted for herring; sometimes it could be reckoned at the same value as coalfish (saithe)[164] or ling.[165] In the spring of 1583 Steven Arnot of Crail and George Bell of Fisherrow prepared a venture. They had received (or were to receive) £44 from John Hamilton of Edinburgh, to whom they obliged themselves to deliver 1,500 keiling.[166] Some days earlier the two partners had promised to deliver to George Corstorphine of Crail 1,000 'fres leinges' (fresh ling) caught off Shetland. Their working capital was to be paid to them by 15 August, which means that they would be fishing off Shetland in late summer or early autumn.[167]

Other kinds of fish related to keiling were sometimes mentioned. Coalfish or saithe was mainly sold as dry fish, the same pertained to ling, although we even saw that this was not always the case. Other kinds were 'gvdlyngis' (good ling ?),[168] skate,[169] and pike,[170] which as a freshwater fish must have been caught inland.

Once, pickled herring is mentioned,[171] apparently a quality different from the usual cured herring Flemish bind. Twice we find smaller barrels ('ye small bynd') than the standard Flemish barrel.[172] Pale herring was decidedly an inferior quality; today pale haddock means smoked, but uncoloured haddock,[173] but in the 16th century in the older Scottish language 'pale' or rather 'palie' or 'peill' meant 'underdeveloped' or 'of inferior size'.[174] The standard description of herring from Northern Scotland was as follows, 'guid and sufficient herring to be Godwilling tane and slane in ye north partes of this realme full pakit and Flemis bind and sufficient merchand wair without any peill herring.'[175] Clearly, the nets would catch herring of different sizes, but only herring of full size was wanted.

### The methods of fishing

As one might imagine, the different kinds of fish were caught according to different methods. Herring were taken in a net suspended from a line between the boat and a buoy ('bow'), which had been laid out.[176]

Keiling, ling and similar kinds of fish, however, were caught on handlines, which could be suspended like the nets from a line between the boat and the buoy, or the line could be held by hand. There was a distinction between the 'grethyng' and the 'smallyng'. The former was a long line used in deep sea fishing for cod and ling, whereas the latter was used by inshore fishermen in order to catch small fish.[177] Different kinds of hooks belonged to the two categories of line.[178] 'Laid stones' (leaden weights) were used to keep the line tight.[179]

About 1500 the buss of the Low Countries appeared for the first time off Shetland.[180] Their great advantage was their size, which allowed them to prepare the herring on board. Consequently, they could stay at sea for longer periods, and smaller vessels would bring them victuals, barrels and salt and take the cured fish back to land, where it was packed. The smaller Scottish vessels had less room on board, thus the preparation of the fish had to take place on the shore.[181] Probably, this curing was provisional, as we learn from Robert Alexander's partnership with Alan Cunningham. The latter was to charter a vessel, with which Robert Alexander would sail to the herring fisheries off Northern Scotland. On his return the partners would divide out the load between them, and Cunningham was to have ready the necessary salt, barrels and part of the 'stuiting' (props for support of the vessel on land).[182] Because of the distance from Northern Scotland to Crail the fish could not be left without cure; consequently, it must have undergone a provisional preparation. Thus in any case, and not only when fishing in the Firth of Forth was concerned, the final cure of the catch would take place at Crail. Here one may ask, whether or not the final cure of the fish caught by the Dutch buss also took place on land where the fish was packed? It is difficult to believe that the quality control took place on board.

At the fishing grounds far from home the fish would be cleaned and provisionally cured by members of the crew, but at Crail it could be the work of women specialists. Thus at Crail William Morton and Charles Blair were obliged to pay 30s. to Margaret Dingwall and Janet Holeis for the 'gutting' (cleaning) of herring.[183]

The packing in barrels would take place at Crail, but we do not know whether it was done by the vessel's crew or if outside helpers were engaged. When the packing was at Crail, a duty had to be paid. A freeman (burgess of Crail) was in 1580 charged 20s. or £1 per last, others three times this amount.[184]

Two years later, the town council realised that large quantities of herring had been landed and packed at Crail and decided to levy a duty in order to finance the repair of the harbour mole. Thus a burgess was to pay 6s. 8d. per last of herring, others 30s. plus £3 per last for the production. Burgesses in partnership with non-burgesses were to pay 40s.[185] In January 1582/3 the price of packing was mentioned as 4d. per barrel and the 'satting' (probably storage) as ½d.[186] In May 1583 the export customs for herring were fixed at 8d. per barrel, if it belonged to a freeman, if not, at 6s. or nine times as much. For oil the figures were 3d. and 6d. respectively.[187] As early as 1570, a non-burgess had had to pay 6s. customs per last of herring,[188] and in spite of the fact that in 1571 the bailies increased the customs dues for three years, this amount was not changed.[189] An additional fee was paid by strangers for the use of the harbour. Thus in November 1570 William Burnesyde of Anstruther acknowledged a debt of 6s. 8d. to the customs officer at Crail, because twice he had anchored there in order to unload his vessel.[190]

**Dry fish**

A number of entries from the 1570s and 1580s deal with dry fish, but sometimes neither the kind of fish nor its price is given. A few contracts refer to the purchase of dry fish. The obligations were registered in spring and the fish was to be delivered in August-September; these facts could indicate that the dry fish came from Shetland. Here the ships fetched dry fish from the end of July to the middle of October.[191] The delivery to James Wilson in July 1590 of 50 dry ling points in the same direction.[192]

Among the kinds of dry fish mentioned we find 'sheills' (?)[193] and coalfish (skaithe). Thirty-one dozen of skaithe were taken, when a vessel belonging to the Englishman Walter Dowlis was plundered at Loch Carron in 1569. The quantity appears too large to have served as victuals for the crew. Probably then the skaithe had been bought at Shetland before Dowlis sailed to Loch Carron.[194]

Ling and keiling were important in the fisheries off Shetland; in the 17th century they and skate were the principal kinds of fish caught other than herring. The Shetland fisheries for keiling took place from the middle of April to the beginning of August, off the Faroes the season was from April to September. The Shetland summer fisheries for ling began about 1 June and ended three months later.[195]

If we can trust the entries in the burgh court books, the price of dry fish varied a great deal. In April 1581 David Vtyng obliged himself to deliver by Easter 1582 one dozen dry keiling to James Norie of St Andrews for £3-18,[196] and on 25 June 1583 Robert Burnie was obliged to pay to John Kingow 14s. for one dozen of dry keiling.[197]

On one occasion we read about 'blawn' (blown) ling and keiling. The fish was briefly salted and hung up to dry in a windy place out of the sun.[198] Three good blown keiling and three good blown ling fetched altogether in 1589 the price of £3.[199]

Alexander Kynnaird's and John Eldis's debt to Alexander Kay of St Andrews – £69 and one dozen dry ling and keiling – probably does not refer to fisheries, but to a trading venture, where Alexander Kay furnished dry fish plus a sum for which other goods were to be purchased.[200]

## The quantities

No source allows us to calculate the exact extent of Crail's fisheries. However, the obligations entered in the burgh court books mention the quantities which the mariners and fishermen promised to deliver to the furnishers of capital some months later (Tables 20-21). Three *caveats* must be considered: the quantities are normative, ie we do not know whether or not they were actually delivered and in due time. Further, the entries refer to fisheries far away; very seldom does an obligation deal with fishing in the Firth of Forth. Finally, the quantities mentioned in the burgh court books must be considered as minima; ventures which needed no borrowed working capital were not registered in the burgh court books.

Until 1600, the beginning of the year was 25 March in Scotland. Here as in the other tables of this work the dates have been arranged according to the modern year, which begins on 1 January. The year is the year in which the promised fish should be delivered and not that in which the obligation was registered. Thus if for instance in September 1580 two mariners obliged themselves to deliver a last of herring each, one at Christmas 1580 and the other on 2 February 1580/1, the former will figure under 1580, the latter under 1581.

In all probability the mixed destinations, which we find in 1569 (Loch Carron or Northern Scotland) and in 1581 (Isles or Northern Scotland) mean that at the time of the contract the mariner was not certain that he could catch the promised quantity at Loch Carron or at the Isles and that consequently he could be obliged to find the fish somewhere else off the coast of Northern Scotland. This circumstance could also explain the dominating role of Northern Scotland in the tables.

The customs accounts allow us to appraise the total of fish legally cleared. Unfortunately, only a few customs books have survived, and moreover, they pertain not only to Crail, but to Anstruther and Pittenweem as well. Consequently, only in a few cases is it possible to distinguish an inhabitant of Crail from those of the other two burghs. As in several cases the mariners and fishermen of Crail worked partly for merchants of other towns, especially Edinburgh, their catch might have been cleared in these towns. The customs accounts of Crail, Anstruther and Pittenweem are all kept in the National Archives of Scotland; they cover the years 1557, 1566, most of the 1570s, and 1582.[201] In addition, a fragmentary account from Crail alone survives from 1620. This one is perhaps worth citing at length as it shows us a more complete glimpse of the trade of the town in isolation from its neighbours. In October a ship of Edinburgh and three vessels of the Low Countries left Crail with coal bound for Flanders and in six voyages four vessels brought timber to Crail from Norway. The *Grace of God* of Pittenweem was cleared in April (no day is given) and again in June 1620, the *Grace of God* of Fisherrow on 13 June and 28 July, the other two ships on 20 and 27 July. The *Grace of God* of Fisherrow was a bark; in June its master was Robert Clark, in July he was mentioned as the merchant with Gavin Fall as the master. In April Robert Smyth was the master and merchant of the bark the *Grace of God* of Pittenweem, in June her master and merchant was James Cook.[202] Thus the vessels were sometimes chartered by the master and/or merchant for only one voyage.

In the customs books sometimes a word or a figure is missing; in these cases the sum of the page given in the account is taken. If, however, this differs from the sum of the individual entries, these have been preferred (Table 3).

The account which begins on 17 December 1574 shows us that the declared herring had been caught in Loch Carron, off Lewis or in the Firth of Forth,[203] whereas most of the herring entered November 1576-November 1577 had been caught in Loch Broom or in the Firth of Forth.[204] Very few persons mentioned in the obligations registered in the burgh court books, appear among those who declared herring from Loch Broom.[205]

In September 1576 George Peirson obliged himself to deliver five lasts of herring from Northern Scotland by Christmas of the same year,[206] but the Cocket Book mentions under his name only two lasts of Loch Broom herring.[207] Two of the five lasts Peirson owed to a merchant of Kirkcaldy, which might have been cleared at the customs office of this town; the remaining three lasts he owed to inhabitants of Crail. This confirms the hypothesis that the obligations referred to the vague expression of 'Northern Scotland' in order to avoid legal difficulties, if herring was not to be found in sufficient quantities in Loch Broom or at one of the specific fishing grounds.

According to the Cocket Book, Ninian Wod declared four lasts of Loch Broom herring,[208] but the burgh court book registers only obligations to deliver to him a total of two lasts and a half of herring from Northern Scotland by Christmas 1577.[209] If Ninian Wod did not himself engage in active fishing, it is probable that his debtors brought him herring from Loch Broom.

Some of the mariners and fishermen who obliged themselves to deliver herring caught off Northern Scotland[210] were also active in the Firth of Forth. Often the quantities declared between November 1576 and November 1577 were considerably larger than those mentioned in their obligations (Table 4).[211]

Only two customs accounts give the date of the clearances of herring. Among 15 clearances one took place on 16 January, four on the first four days of March, the rest in February.[212] As a rule, for herring from Northern Scotland the date of delivery was Christmas; here the dates indicate that the fish could have been caught in Loch Broom or Loch Carron.

In 1557, herring was cleared between 25 February and 15 March, which indicates that herring from Loch Broom or Loch Carron could have been meant.[213] Keiling (cod) was mainly entered at the end of

February and in April;[214] as at Shetland and the Faroes the fisheries for keiling began in April,[215] these clearances could refer to fish caught somewhere else. As frequently keiling could be delivered instead of herring, the keiling registered could have been caught off Northern Scotland.

Two accounts mention considerable quantities of fish entered as pieces and not as barrels, but the kind of fish is not mentioned. This could mean that only part of the catch had been packed when it was declared at the customs office.

Because of the fairly close economic relations between the East Neuk and both Dundee and Edinburgh, one would expect that part of the fish caught by the mariners of Crail might have been declared in one of these burghs. As the home town of the persons declaring the goods are not always mentioned, their identification must necessarily be tentative. Moreover, sometimes residents of Crail and Anstruther are grouped together in the customs accounts With these *caveats* in mind we arrive at the following figures for herring declared at Dundee by residents of Crail (Table 5).[216]

For Edinburgh the corresponding figures are given in Table 6. Included here are the merchants of Edinburgh who worked with contractors of Crail. On the basis of the customs accounts from Crail, Dundee and Edinburgh an estimate can be given of the quantities of herring declared, but again, it must be remembered that these must be considered as minima (Table 7). Although the figures given in Table 7 are not complete (because of the missing customs accounts), they clearly show Crail's dominating role in the herring fisheries in the second half of the 16th century.

CHAPTER 4

# The reckoning

## The cost of a last of herring

We already know that the furnishers of capital lent the skippers money which was to be paid back in fish some months later. For certain years we can calculate the average value of a last of herring, but these figures must be treated with caution (Table 8). First, they are estimates in advance, referring to the possible outcome of the fishing season, and moreover, they are the result of negotiations, perhaps even haggling, between the skipper and the furnisher of capital.[217]In 1583, the average estimated value of a last of herring was £25-14-8 or £27-9-10, disregarding two very low estimates of £12 and £17 respectively. The credits furnished by Alan Cunningham are illustrative (Table 9).

The four entries here are comparable in most respects: the obligation was registered at the end of August or in September, the term of payment was Christmas and the herring was to be caught off Northern Scotland. Nevertheless, the estimated value of the fish was considerably lower in the case of a joint venture with two participants. In this way, Cunningham divided his risk and could thus afford to yield a cheap credit. If only one of the venturers fulfilled his obligation, Cunningham would obtain a gain, if both did it, his profit would amount to at least 100%.

The estimated value of a last of herring was composed of several elements. Barrels were of course needed, and we saw that in most years the price of a last of Flemish barrels lay between £4 and £5 (Table 2). However, the gutted and salted herring shrunk and consequently had to be repacked at land. Out of 14 barrels the final last of 12 barrels would come. In order to salt a last of herring, ie 14 barrels at sea, four barrels of salt would be needed. A last of barrels would logically contain 14 barrels.[218] As, in 1578, 20 barrels of small (ie Scottish) salt were sold for £15,[219] four barrels necessary to salt a last of herring would cost £3.

Information concerning the value of the equipment is scanty. We only know that in 1559 a herring net was estimated at 40d. or 3s. 4d.,[220] which does not correspond to Martin Rorke's statement that in the last third of the 16th century the value of a fishing boat was *c* £60 and £3 for a net,[221] though perhaps the boats took on board a set of nets worth in total the latter sum.

If the owner of a ship took part in the venture, he would often put his vessel at the disposal of the partners; in the burgh court books of Crail the crear is the most frequently mentioned type. It held 30-50 tons;[222] according to the Dundee shipping lists, ships returned from the Western Isles with 15 to 25 lasts of herring, but in 1586 a vessel of Crail which could load only 10 lasts had been fishing off the Northern Hebrides.[223]

In some cases the partners would have to charter a ship and to rent the equipment. In 1566/7 a voyage to Loch Broom apparently cost £30 'lyuht mony',[224] some months later, it was estimated at £25.[225] In October 1569, the *Martin* was let with full equipment for a voyage to the Northern Isles and back for £20,[226] and in February 1573/4 Thomas Moreis obliged himself to pay to Andro Baxter £4 for the hire of one eighth of his boat for a voyage to Northern Scotland,[227] which means that the charter of the entire boat would have cost £32.

Obviously a voyage to Norway to fetch timber was more expensive; here the charter of a ship would amount to £90 (Table 10).[228]

Towards the end of the 16th century, a fleet of half-deck crears would regularly leave the East Neuk harbours in order to fish off the Western Isles.[229] In 1572, Robert Balcony had 14 lasts of herring in his crear, for which he had to pay customs;[230] in 1576 the possibility was evoked that with his crear George Peirson could catch 15 lasts of herring,[231] but in another case the lower limit of nine lasts was mentioned.[232] In some cases, the crear would continue from the fisheries to France in order to sell her load there.[233]

That the crear was a sea-going vessel is also shown by entries in the Dundee Shipping Lists. We find crears returning from Flanders,[234] from 'Werlindhous' with osmund iron and timber, which would indicate that the vessel had been in Sweden (Lödöse ?),[235] and above all from Norway.[236] The quantities of fish entered at Dundee show us the minimal loading capacity of the vessels (Table 11). Some of the ships carried other goods besides the fish, especially skins and hides, but it would hardly be possible to calculate their volume. For this reason the estimates of loading capacities must be seen as minima.

Among the ships entered at Dundee in 1589 we find a few crears (Table 12) listed among other ships. Excluding the crears, the average loading capacity of these ships would be 17 lasts and nine barrels. We may thus conclude that the crear was a relatively small sea-going ship, of an average loading capacity of perhaps 15 lasts.

It is reasonable to assume that a ship with equipment could be chartered at £30 for a voyage to the fisheries off Northern Scotland or the Hebrides. For a season of fishing at the Northern Isles, a boat with a crew of six would (in the 1790s) need 15 lispunds of meal and 12 pints of spirits, which was supplemented by victuals like butter or milk brought by the crew.[237]

A lispund is about a twelfth of a barrel; 15 lispund would correspond to one barrel and a quarter.[238] We may surmise that in a fisherman's context the herring barrel would have been meant. As we have seen, it held *c* 1.22 hl, at least since 1573. One barrel and a quarter would thus be 1.53 hl.

If we identify 'meal' with oatmeal, which appears reasonable because of its role in the staple Scottish diet, we can calculate approximately the value of this amount of oatmeal. Prior to 1696, the wheat boll was used also for oatmeal. The standard measure was the boll of Linlithgow, but the boll of Fife was slightly larger. As the peck is one sixteenth of a boll, a peck of Fife would correspond to 9.095 litres against the Linlithgow peck of 8.785 litres. In 1575, the burgh council of Dunfermline fixed the price of oatmeal at 30d. the peck.[239] This price from Dunfermline in 1575 can be completed by the fiars' prices for Fife, which are known for most of the years in question (Table 13).

Generally, fiars were struck in February and should register the prices at which the victuals had been sold since 1 November.[240] This means that the period represented in the fiars begins two or three months after the harvest and ends before an eventual scarcity began to make itself felt. But, one could object, the ships would leave in September, before the fiars had been struck. True, but as the ships bought their oatmeal immediately after the harvest, the skipper must have been able to see whether or not the harvest of the year had been good. Rather, one would think, the fiars would be slightly higher than the price actually paid immediately after the harvest. For this reason the fiars have not been increased here by 10% as proposed in order to find the approximate market price throughout the year.[241]

The price fixed in 1575 by the council of Dunfermline, 30d. the peck of oatmeal, corresponds to £2 the boll, or exactly half the Fife fiar. The latter was struck as an average for the whole county (thus also, the East Neuk), whereas the Dunfermline price refers to only a single locality in the hinterland of which the harvest could have been particularly rich that year. For this reason, in this study, the fiars are preferred in order to calculate the cost of oatmeal. The 15 lispund or 1.53 hl. would correspond to 16.8 pecks of Fife for the whole ship.

One must query whether brandy played the same role in a fisherman's diet in the 16th century as it was to do in the late 18th century.[242] For this reason it would be more prudent not to consider it a standard item in the equipment of a ship in the late 16th century.

The fishing gear (nets and lines) belonged to the individual fishermen, as shown in the examples mentioned in Chapter One, Equipment. The cost of a ship for a voyage to Northern Scotland can be seen in Table 14.

It appears to be a reasonable estimate, if we reckon that the vessel could load 15 lasts of herring, and if, as it was likely, that Scottish salt was used to cure the herring, the four barrels necessary to salt a last of herring would cost £3. The price of barrels changed from one year to another, as Table 2 tells us. In order to arrive at the production cost of one last of herring one should reckon one fifteenth of the charter of the ship, £3 for salt and the price of oatmeal and a last of barrels.

To these amounts should be added the internal customs duties, which on 1 June 1571 had been fixed by the bailies of Crail at 8d. a last of herring belonging to a freeman (burgess) of Crail, at 1s. 4d. for a last belonging to a freeman from another town, or at 6s. for a last belonging to an unfree man (non-burgess) resident at Crail or elsewhere. When the herring had been commissioned by a merchant living outside Crail, the obligation stipulated very often that the fish should be delivered at Crail. In this way the foreign merchant would have to pay the customs at Crail on outgoing goods.[243]

On land the herring had to be repacked; in January 1582/3 15 barrels were packed at 5s., thus at 4s. the last;[244] on top of that came the duties on the packaging of herring at Crail. According to the ordinance of 20 August 1580 a freeman who had packed his herring at Crail had to pay the duty of 20s. or £1 per last, whereas an unfree man paid three times this amount.[245] Two years later a supplementary duty was introduced in order to finance the repair of the harbour mole. The decree mentioned that recently large quantities of herring had been landed at Crail, where it had been packed. For a freeman the supplementary duty was fixed at 6s. 8d. per last, for an unfree man at 30s. or at £1-10.[246] Moreover, a duty of anchorage was charged, at least from the skippers who did not live at Crail. Thus a skipper of Anstruther had to pay 6s. 8d. for anchoring twice at Crail in order to unload his cargo.[247] For certain years mentioned in Table 14, we know the price of barrels, which allows us to calculate the production costs of a last of herring belonging to a freeman of Crail (Table 15).

Also for certain years, Table 8 gives the estimates of the value of a last of herring. The figures are averages, but as the individual estimates are the outcome of negotiations between the skipper and the furnisher of capital, the averages represent a consensus. For this reason figures which lie well outside the general trend have been disregarded, like those for 1579, 1584, 1589, and 1590 (Table 16).

Although the gross profit can be calculated for only a few years, the figures show that the furnishing of working capital for Crail's herring fishing could be very good business, with profits of over 100%.

Some of the herring caught was exported to England, France or the Baltic region. From 1549, Scottish goods passing through the Sound paid an *ad valorem* duty of 1%[248] consequently, the Sound Toll Accounts reckon the value of the articles carried. If the cargo was correctly declared, this figure would reflect the price free on board in the port of departure.[249] In 1574, 1578 and 1581 some ships carrying herring came from Marstrand, which makes it probable that the herring had been caught there and not in Scotland. Consequently, these vessels have not been considered.

Among the years mentioned in Table 16, Scottish herring appears in the Sound Toll Accounts only in 1568 and 1583. It also occurs in 1589-90. Because of inflation in both Scotland and Denmark, the rate of exchange between the two currencies is difficult to find, at least as far as the first year is concerned. For 1583 we know that one daler was the equivalent of £2 WScots;[250] and in May 1590 the old daler still had a value of £2 Scots.[251] According to a royal decree of 28 March 1573, the Sound Toll could be paid only in gold or in old daler.[252] No Scottish herring was cleared at Elsinore in 1584, but for 1583 and 1589-90 we find its value declared at the Sound Toll (Table 17) and these figures can be compared with the estimated values given in Table 8 (Table 18).

We have been able to calculate the profits in two phases of the herring's progress from the sea to the consumer's table. In the production phase – catch, cure and packing – the furnishers of capital could as a rule obtain profits of between 100% and 200%. Most of them were locally based and would seldom export their fish, but sell them at Crail or in the surrounding countryside.

A few furnishers of capital were based in towns other than Crail, mainly in Edinburgh or in other burghs in the East Neuk. We cannot exclude the possibility that they also acquired the herring in order to supply a local market. In some cases, however, the external merchant probably bought herring from Crail merchants in order to export it. That profit was added on the way from the local merchant to the exporting merchant is seen from Table 18. The profits were considerable, but not as exorbitant as in the phase of production. On its final way to the consumer, the herring would pass through one or two more phases: sale in the port abroad to a merchant, who, if he was a wholesale trader, would sell it to a retailer, from whom the consumer would buy it. In either case a profit would be added, but here our Scottish sources are silent.

## Indemnities and interests

We have seen that the value of a last of herring was an estimate at which the skipper and the furnisher of capital arrived through negotiations. If little or no fish was to be had, the money advanced had to be paid back, either in whole or in part. But it could happen that during the voyage the mariner found that the price of herring was likely to prove higher than the one agreed. In this case the mariner could be tempted to sell his catch at this higher price, and to tell the furnisher of capital that no fish could be caught while just paying back the amount received.

As a guarantee against this type of abuse, several contracts contain the clause that the equivalent of the highest market price, and not only the amount advanced, should be paid back.

In most cases the market price was not specified,[253] but a few contracts mention which market was to be considered: that of Crail between Christmas and Easter,[254] that of Edinburgh or Leith,[255] the highest market price in Scotland or France,[256] or in Scotland, England or France.[257] Consequently, the mariner would find no advantage in pretending that no fish could be had, not even by selling his catch abroad.

Besides the payment of the highest market price, another system of indemnities was used; we find it eg in a contract between Arthur Gray of Crail and Steven Balfour of St Andrews. The latter had given Gray £48 Scots, and Gray was to deliver to Balfour 18 barrels of Forth herring. If no fish was to be had, the sum received was to be paid back; if there was herring but Gray did not deliver the agreed 18 barrels, he was to pay Balfour £57 Scots, ie the amount received plus an indemnity of £9 (10s. the barrel) or 18.75 %.[258] This was not the only case, and in Table 19 similar indemnities have been calculated.

These must have been defined through negotiations between the furnisher of capital and the mariner. However, the individual indemnities varied a great deal, and if the indemnity was modest, the mariner would perhaps be able to sell his fish at a higher price than agreed and still make a profit in spite of the indemnity. Then the other system with the payment of the highest market price was fairer, less complicated and guaranteed that the creditor could get his fish, even if he should buy it in the market.

Two cases from July 1569 stipulate that the mariner should pay his creditor, Ninian Hamilton, a certain amount for each voyage. Alexander Airth acknowledged his debt of £50 Scots and agreed to pay £4 for each voyage, whereas James Dawson owed Hamilton £60 Scots and obliged himself to pay £5 for each voyage, thus 8 % and 8.3 % respectively.[259] In all likelihood, these amounts should be considered as interest, because the mariners did not settle their accounts with Hamilton at the end of each voyage, but kept the loan as working capital for the future voyages as well.

Apparently, there was no fixed rate of interest (or at any rate not one which was observed). On 26 September 1568, John Bownie recognized his debt of £12 to John Beane, which was due on 11 November. If the amount had not been paid by Christmas, another pound would be due, thus an interest of 8.3 %.[260] Two days earlier, on 24 September William Arnit acknowledged his debt of £60-14-0 to Patrick Lindsay due on 11 November. If the sum had not been paid by Christmas, interest of 25 % was to be paid as well.[261]

# CHAPTER 5

# The participants in the fisheries

## The mariner contractors

By 'contractors' we mean the mariners who went to sea and returned home two or three months later with the catch. Frequently one or more merchants advanced them working capital, to be paid back in fish. Often the contractor worked alone, but also frequently in company with others. A partnership with one contractor did by no means exclude a merchant from collaboration with another. We have, for example, seen that in 1590 Thomas Beane in partnership with William Hunter sent salt and claret to Shetland and at the same time was in partnership with John Corstorphine with whom he also sent English beer to Shetland, while Beane himself set out for another voyage.[262]

Partnerships appear to have been more frequent in the late 1560s than later on; perhaps Crail's engagement in the herring fishing was fairly recent in the 1560s, and only when more experience had been obtained, were the fishermen and mariners prepared to work on their own. Sometimes a partnership worked with more than one merchant; thus in 1570 Andro Corstorphine and Andro Peirson obliged themselves to deliver to Thomas Hall of Prestonpans two lasts of herring[263] and some days later promised to give 10 barrels of herring to Patrick Lindsay.[264] Also James Cass, James Dingwall, and John Martin formed a partnership in 1576, working for Patrick Hogg of Kirkcaldy as well as for Walter Ballingall of Crail.[265]

The customs accounts of Crail (with Anstruther and Pittenweem) yield information supplementing that of the burgh court books. As sometimes, in the accounts, two or more people are mentioned with the goods declared, it is reasonable to believe that those mentioned were the owners of the goods. The circumstance that the same person might be mentioned under different dates of the same month again points to him as the owner of the goods and not as the skipper.

In 1566 Alexander Ramsay and Patrick Lindsay cleared 12 lasts of herring,[266] but we never find Patrick Lindsay as a contractor, only as a merchant, and the same applies to Ramsay.[267] This means that in this case no obligation was entered, which does not exclude Ramsay's partnership with Lindsay.

Sometimes the quantities mentioned in the customs accounts exceed those commissioned by the merchants. This suggests that the contractors either had received orders which had not been registered in the burgh court books or that they ventured on their own as well.

Even if a contractor had received a working capital corresponding to the value of the catch, the latter legally belonged to him. In spite of the amount received and of the obligation to pay it with a quantity of fish, the contractor could sell his fish at a higher price to somebody else and pay the received amount back. In order to circumvent this the obligations frequently stated that in such a case the equivalent of the highest market price should be paid.

A look at the contractors' obligations (Tables 20-1) shows us that they did not participate in the fisheries every year. Cases like Robert Arnot (six consecutive years 1576-81) or Robert Dingwall (five years 1579-83) were rare. Fishing in the north appears to have been only one among several possible activities, and it was undertaken only in promising years.

Moreover, the customs accounts from the district of Crail, Anstruther and Pittenweem show clearly that the obligations to deliver certain quantities represented only part of the contractors' activities. Further, they yield information on years not covered by the obligations. Sometimes unspecified 'English' or 'Norway' goods were entered, which must refer to goods imported from these countries. Also Norway 'stuling' (ie cargo) appears, as a rule salt and cloth, which must have been articles exported from Scotland to Norway. Table 22 combines the information given in Table 21 with that of the customs accounts.

Several contractors mentioned in Table 22 must have sailed to England with part of their catch, which consequently would have been cleared in an English port. Moreover, sometimes the fish caught by the contractors of Crail was landed in another Scottish port, especially Dundee or Leith. As the names given in the customs accounts are those of the owners of the goods, we find both mariner contractors and merchants in these records. We saw that in 1566/7 the two merchants, Patrick Lindsay of Crail and Alexander Ramsay of Dundee entered 12 lasts of herring, besides which Ramsay declared two lasts of Loch Broom herring and Lindsay nine barrels of unspecified herring.[268] Other inhabitants of Crail also landed their goods at Dundee (Table 23).

For our purpose the customs accounts of Edinburgh are more difficult to handle, as they give only the name of the person declaring the goods and not his town of residence. Although aware of the risk, an attempt has been made to identify certain persons whom we find in the Edinburgh customs accounts with certain contractors or merchants of Crail (see Table 20). The result is given in Table 24.

The customs accounts of Dundee and Edinburgh show that herring caught by contractors of Crail might well be landed at Dundee, above all during the early part of the period under investigation, whereas fish was seldom declared at Edinburgh, and this in spite of the numerous contracts which obliged the contractors of Crail to furnish fish to the merchants of the capital. Rather they would enter hides and skins, which were traditional Scottish export goods. Moreover, they declared important quantities of cloth, but from the customs accounts we cannot see whether or not they refer to Scottish cloth or to cloth imported from abroad. The other goods mentioned appear to refer mainly to trade within Scotland; it is thus probable that the inhabitants of Crail took the goods from the regions of production in Scotland to the bigger cities, where the local merchants would take care of the further distribution, eventually sending them abroad. At any rate, we see that the fisheries and the trade in fish were only one among several economic activities of the inhabitants of Crail, but also that several contractors had obliged themselves to merchants of Edinburgh or the Canongate (Table 20).

Besides England, Norway was another important trading partner for Crail. Salt and cloth were the main exports across the North Sea from Scotland and in return wood and timber were imported into Scotland.

As a rule, the obligations registered in the burgh court books refer to herring Flemish bind, of internationally recognised standard, or as the contemporary wording had it: '...guid and sufficient herring to be Godwilling tane and slane in ye north partes of this realme full pakit and flemis bind and sufficient merchand wair without any peill herring...'[269] In this way the merchant kept open the possibility of export.

Herring caught within the Firth of Forth also played a significant role, especially in the 1570s.[270] Also, fairly big quantities of 'pale herring', an inferior quality, were landed at Crail, Anstruther or Pittenweem. The juxtaposition of the customs accounts and the obligations entered in the burgh court books shows us that fishing was more important in the economy of the contractors than one would believe from the obligations alone, although trading in fish seldom became a full time occupation.

**The career of a mariner contractor: Arthur Gray**

Obviously, although participation in a partnership did not preclude a fisherman or a mariner from working individually, it was a means to reduce the individual risk. In 1577, John Bruce and Arthur Gray obliged themselves to deliver half a last of herring to Patrick Lindsay, and at the same time Gray promised to deliver one last and a half to Margaret Cornwall and six barrels to Andro Lindsay.[271]

Arthur Gray is particularly interesting, because we can follow his engagement in fishing over a fairly long period. In 1569, he was working in Loch Carron together with Andro Baxter, Patrick Dyk and Thomas Howat on board a ship belonging to John Davidson of Crail. He must have been involved in the spoliation of an English vessel; the Scottish skipper, James Davidson, had been obliged to pay £21 and now sued Baxter, Gray and Howat for their share of the amount.[272]

Although in 1569 Gray had worked for somebody else or with his own capital, in 1570 he received from William Arnot £26 in September in view of a voyage to Northern Scotland; in return he promised to deliver to Arnot a last of herring by 13 January 1570/1. If no herring was to be had, Arnot was ready to accept keiling, otherwise the sum was to be paid back.[273] The venture must have been encouraging, as in 1571 Gray made an agreement on similar terms with Thomas Clark.[274]

This was a modest beginning, and Gray must have earned most of his livelihood by other activities, for instance as a mariner on board a ship belonging to somebody else. By 1574 he had been admitted a burgess of Crail and would thus have to pay less customs than unfreemen. In September he registered a debt to William Bruce of £23 to be paid by Christmas;[275] the date could indicate an engagement in the autumn fishing, but a voyage abroad should not be excluded.

In May 1576 Gray and Andro Davidson recognised a debt of £34-10 to be paid to William Corstorphine by 15 September. On the following day Davidson admitted a debt of £121-4 to Thomas Browne in the 'Mwirhouse' to be paid by 8 September.[276] The dates could allude to a planned voyage to Shetland, in which Davidson was the leading partner.

In the autumn fishing off Northern Scotland of the same year, Gray engaged himself as he had done in 1570-1. He agreed to deliver to Margaret Cornwall 18 barrels of herring in return for £46 and to William Melville one last for £32, in each case by Christmas.[277]

In 1577 Gray appears to have taken part in an enterprise in spring; he recognised debts of £23 to Margaret Cornwall and of £20 to Walter Ballingall, both to be paid by 15 August.[278] As in neither case fish is mentioned, Gray might have borrowed the money for a trading voyage,[279] eg to Shetland, which would correspond with the dates. At the same time, he obliged himself to deliver a last of herring from Northern Scotland to Patrick Lindsay by Christmas. Apparently, he received no working capital, which means that Gray would be paid only at the delivery of the fish.[280]

Gray then again engaged himself in the autumn fisheries; Margaret Cornwall had lent him an unspecified sum, for which he should deliver her 18 barrels of herring from Northern Scotland by Christmas or pay back the amount received.[281] A week later he recognized his debt of £23-6-8 to Andro Lindsay, to be paid by Christmas in the form of half a last of herring from Northern Scotland.[282] With John Bruce he promised to provide Patrick Lindsay with half a last of herring from Northern Scotland; Lindsay must have given them an unspecified working capital, but if they failed they should pay him the equivalent of the highest market price.[283] Moreover, Gray borrowed £46 from Thomas Browne in the 'Mwirhouse' to be repaid by Candlemas (2 February), 1577/8.[284]

In spite of these preparations, Gray must have been unable to provide Patrick Lindsay with the herring which he had promised him in April. On the last day of November he obliged himself to pay by Christmas £42 to Lindsay as the price of a last of herring.[285]

In 1578 and 1579 Gray must have sought his fortune elsewhere, perhaps in Scottish shipping abroad, but in November 1579 he promised to deliver 16 barrels of herring from Northern Scotland to William Hunter by Christmas 1580.[286] In this way he could find his fish either in the spring or in the autumn. In May 1580 he obliged himself to provide Patrick Hogg of Kirkcaldy with half a last of herring from Northern Scotland by Martinmas (11 November) 1580 or to pay the equivalent of the highest market price.[287]

The calendar of Gray's engagements shows us that providing fish must have been only one of his activities, which could have been supplemented by other forms of shipping or international trade. From 1581 he appears to have concentrated on the fish trade all year round, and probably at that time he acquired a crear.

In the spring of 1581 he again obliged himself to furnish herring from Northern Scotland by Christmas, one last to William Morton and one to James Woid.[288] In August he agreed with Mr John Harte of the Canongate to provide him with a last of herring from Northern Scotland by Christmas and William Morton, who was a cooper, declared that Gray would deliver to him a last of herring from Northern Scotland;[289] perhaps Morton stood surety for Gray's payment. At the same time Gray promised James Summerville of Edinburgh to provide him with two lasts of herring from Northern Scotland by Christmas or to pay the equivalent of the highest market price.[290]

In November 1581 Gray contracted obligations to deliver herring from Northern Scotland at the end of the winter. Edward Gryge by 1 March was to receive six barrels of herring,[291] and with Thomas Beane, younger and John Paterson and Arthur Gray was to pay to William Hunter of Crail £80 along with three and a half barrels of herring by 27 February 1581/2.[292] Again in partnership with John Paterson, he had received £60 as working capital from Mr John Harte of the Canongate. In return he was to receive two lasts of herring from Northern Scotland by 1 March 1581/2; if no herring was to be had, they could give him keiling, but then as an indemnity they had to pay an extra barrel per last or altogether 26 barrels. If neither were available, the money was to be paid back.[293]

Next time, working alone, Gray obliged himself to deliver to John Summerville of Edinburgh two lasts of herring from Northern Scotland by 1 March 1581/2 in return for £60 received. If he got herring without providing Summerville with the two lasts, he was to pay the equivalent of the highest market price.[294]

In the spring of 1582 Gray promised William Morton of Crail a last of herring from the 'Isles of Northern Scotland' by Christmas, if he failed, he was to pay the equivalent of the highest market price.[295]

We do not know all Gray's activities in the spring and summer of 1582, but apparently he did not participate in the summer fishing or trade at Shetland. He could have worked as a carrier, but if so, we do not know where he went. At any rate, he took part in the autumn fishing that year, borrowing from William Powstay £46 and from James Ogilvie £38, both to be paid back by Christmas.[296] Moreover, he had promised Alan Cunningham a last of herring and Ninian Woid six and a half lasts of herring, both from Northern Scotland and both by Christmas. If no herring was to be had, the received working capital of unspecified amount had to be paid back; if there was herring and Gray did not deliver it, he must pay the equivalent of the highest market price.[297] The same conditions pertained to Gray's obligation in partnership with John Browne to provide John Macmoran of Edinburgh with 18 barrels of herring from Northern Scotland: as working capital they had received £51.[298]

Gray intended to send his own crear to the autumn fishing off Northern Scotland; William Robertson of Crail promised by Christmas to provide Mr John Harte of the Canongate one last of herring from Arthur Gray's crear.[299] The vessel would thus, Gray could hope, be loaded with 10 lasts of herring, which was the total amount to be delivered to the persons who had ordered it. If, however, such a ship could load 15 lasts (see Chapter 2, section Northern Scotland), the crear would have had room for five more lasts. Did Gray hope to find sufficient herring to get a full load? Or was he prepared to sail with only 10 lasts? The sources give us no answer.

The next year became critical for Gray. In February 1582/3 he promised to provide Steven Balfour of St Andrews with 18 barrels of herring from the Firth of Forth by 8 September. He had in advance received £48, but if herring was to be had and Gray did not deliver it, he must pay £57.[300]

A month later Gray received from Ninian Woid a total of more than £100. In return Gray sold him half of his crear, the *Harry*, with equipment. Actually this was a pledge, because until 8 September, Gray could buy back the sold half by repaying the amount received.[301] We do not know his activities in the spring or the summer of 1583, but the possibility had been left open for him to redeem the pledge and to participate in the autumn fishing. He must have planned to do so; in September he borrowed £33-15 from James Woid, son of the late Andro Woid of Largo, for which sum Gray agreed to deliver 18 barrels of herring from Northern Scotland by Christmas.[302]

Gray's economic difficulties must have increased and in all likelihood he was unable to pay his debts to John Summerville of Edinburgh and to Mr James Harte of the Canongate. At least since 1581 he had been involved in business relations with them, and probably in 1583 Harte had lent him £125, to be repaid by 3 March 1583/4. At the end of January it was clear that Gray would be unable to pay the whole sum, so his sureties, Thomas and William Robertson of Crail paid £57 on his behalf.[303]

An arrangement was also found with John Summerville. Gray still owed him £50 from an earlier debt, which he was allowed to pay in two instalments, £26 by 8 September and the rest at Christmas. The notice has been crossed through in the source, indicating that the debt had been paid.[304] Gray does not appear in the burgh court books any more (but the years 1584 to 1588/9 are missing); perhaps the payments of 1584 should be seen as measures to liquidate his business.

Gray's career is interesting. He appears to have been a mariner, who for several years worked on board somebody else's ship. Prudently, he accepted smaller orders of herring, as a rule receiving a working capital to pay back in fish. Gradually he became ever more involved in the fishing; until 1580 he participated only in the autumn fishing, but appears to have traded with Shetland during the fisheries in spring and early summer.

The huge profits to be earned in fishing must have caused him to dedicate himself to fishing full time from 1581, and at the same time he must have acquired a crear. However, profits changed; in 1582 they were, although still substantial, only half of what they had been the year before. It proved unwise to concentrate on one kind of business; moreover, his acquisition of the crear as the only owner could have strained his credit too far. His business collapsed in 1583; he came to an arrangement with his principal creditors, but the sources do not allow us to see whether or not his business managed to recover.

**Other mariner contractors**

Most contractors worked only as such, but a small number appear also among the merchants. Thus we find George Corstorphine as a contractor in 1569, 1571 and 1576 and as a merchant in 1583.[305] Probably he had given up active shipping and remained at home.

Thus in some cases the frontier between the contractor and the merchant was variable, and sometimes the merchant would assume the role of a contractor working for another merchant. He would get the working capital and would have to organise the voyage and in due time deliver the quantity of fish agreed upon, but in all probability he would stay at home waiting for the vessel to return.

In the same way, the organising role could be taken over by an experienced mariner, as we see with Alexander Farmer in 1573. From John Melville he had received £58 in return for which he was to deliver two lasts of herring. Eighteen barrels should be taken from William Annand's crear and six from that belonging to Andro Baxter.[306] Apparently, Farmer was to arrange with the crews of the two vessels that part of the catch should be reserved for him, who probably did not sail with them.

As the fishing was seasonal, one could have expected many of the mariners and fishermen to take part in it every year, which was certainly not the case with the contractors, as a glance at the catalogue tells us. In the introduction we mentioned the fishing seasons, which made it possible for a fisherman to work all year round except for the winter months of January and February. It must be remembered, however, that fishing was only one of a mariner's several possible activities. Apparently in certain years the skippers found it more profitable to use the vessel for other trades than fishing, though the latter activity must have been especially promising in Loch Carron in 1569 and off Northern Scotland in 1576.

Some of the contractors we find in the Sound Toll Accounts of Elsinore. In this source the nationality is that of the goods and the person in charge is the skipper.[307] In 1562 Andro Davidson elder of Crail passed Elsinore on his return voyage from Königsberg[308] and in 1576 George Peirson ('Jørgen Paterson') of Crail arrived at Elsinore on 24 May with his ship in ballast. About five weeks later he cleared at Elsinore on his way back from Danzig with rye and tar.[309] Peirson thus found time for a Baltic voyage before the autumn fisheries.

William Annand, whom we mainly see as a merchant, also made a voyage to the Baltic, in 1578. On 22 April he cleared at Elsinore with four lasts of Scottish herring and nine barrels of train-oil, and on 24 May called again at Elsinore on his way back from Königsberg with rye, flax and naval stores on board.[310]

Among the contractors who sailed to the Baltic as skippers we find William Lyall. In 1577 he came from Crail with French wine, stale herring and a piece of kersey; he returned from Königsberg with flax, naval stores and Swedish iron.[311] Again in 1580, before the autumn fishing, he made a voyage to the Baltic. From Crail he came with salt; on his way back he had Swedish iron and rye on board which would indicate a Prussian port of departure (Danzig or Königsberg). Before arriving at Elsinore he had called at Copenhagen, which could mean that part of his cargo was bound for the capital of Denmark and that in this respect he had worked as a carrier.[312]

William Daw we find as a contractor in 1577 and 1589. In 1580, coming from Crail he passed Elsinore with French wine, train-oil, cloth and skins and returned from Königsberg with Swedish iron, flax and naval stores.[313] Again in 1583, but with his home town wrongly mentioned as St Andrews, he passed Elsinore with train-oil on board.[314] We do not know where he went nor when he returned, perhaps he sailed through the Great Belt. In 1587 he passed Elsinore in ballast (16 lasts) and returned from Danzig with (at least partly Swedish) iron, tar and pitch, hemp, flax and clapboard.[315] Again in 1589 he passed Elsinore with grocery,[316] and again we do not know when he returned nor from where. We notice that the Baltic voyages took place in late spring – early summer, thus leaving time for the participation in the autumn fisheries.

More enigmatic is Andro Daw, whom we find as a contractor in 1582: he was then established at Largo.[317] He can have been the same person, who in 1570-1 entered 12 lasts of herring.[318] By 1587 he appears to have moved to Crail, as on 1 May a certain Andro Daw of Crail cleared cloth, white leather and coneyskins at Elsinore; a month later he returned from Danzig with rye.[319] Again in 1588 he sailed to the Baltic, this time with herring, skins and cloth at a total value of 157 daler; from Königsberg he brought rope, hemp, flax, iron and tar at the value of 857 daler.[320] Also for him the fish trade was only one of his activities, and again the time of the Baltic voyages would allow him to take part in the autumn fisheries.

The identification of the two skippers Thomas Davidson is not obvious. In 1579 and again in 1581 Thomas Davidson younger is mentioned,[321] but before and after these two years only Thomas Davidson. Probably then Thomas Davidson elder is the person mentioned before 1579 and he must have died after 9 May 1581.

In 1569 the Burgh Court found that John Morton, cooper, should pay Thomas Davidson (elder) for part of the charter of Davidson's ship for a voyage to Norway;[322] two years later, the cooper and the skipper cooperated again on a voyage to Norway.[323] Also in 1569, Davidson took part in the Loch Carron fishing and was involved in the spoliation of an English vessel.[324] This is the only indication of his participation in the fisheries; above all he was a long-distance skipper.

Coming from Flushing with salt and sugar, he cleared at Elsinore on 25 April 1576 and again on 28 May on his return voyage from Danzig with rye, flour, soap, Swedish iron, and naval stores.[325]

In 1578, the two skippers Thomas Davidson passed Elsinore within an interval of two weeks, but any further identification appears impossible. As in this year the interval between two clearances at Elsinore for a voyage to Königsberg would be four to five weeks, it is assumed this is also the interval for the voyages by the skippers Thomas Davidson.

The former arrived at Elsinore from Crail on 10 April with a cargo of herring, foreign and Scottish salt and train-oil, and on 15 May he returned from Königsberg with rye, flax, clapboard and naval stores.[326] Also the other Thomas Davidson came from Crail with Scottish herring, Scottish salt and train-oil, on his return from Königsberg he passed Elsinore with a cargo of rye, tar and pitch.[327]

Again in 1585 Thomas Davidson younger made a Baltic voyage. On 13 May he cleared French wine (Poitou and salt, which could mean that in the autumn of 1584 he had made a voyage to France to load salt and the new wine). He returned from Danzig (with his Christian name wrongly entered as Jacob = James) with tar, Swedish iron, gunpowder, sword blades and copper.[328]

One of the two skippers Thomas Davidson must have been the younger, who in 1579 worked with George Meldrum of Crail. Meldrum owned a ship of which Davidson must have been the master. From Meldrum Davidson had received 18 barrels herring, which he had sold in France.[329] Also on an earlier occasion Meldrum was interested in trade with France, especially with Bordeaux.[330]

Several times we find Thomas Martin, skipper, as a contractor, who was admitted as a burgess of Crail in January 1566/7. At the same time he borrowed money in order to buy part of a ship, the *John*. We also read that in 1566 he had taken part in a summer voyage to Shetland.[331] In 1570/1 he bought from William Kay a quarter part in a Flemish vessel.[332]

In 1576, he stood surety for James Sinclair, *foged* at Shetland,[333] and in the same year he commissioned 18 barrels herring from Northern Scotland but also received commissions.[334] In January 1580/1 we find him as the owner of the *Thomas* that had sailed with herring from the Isles on behalf of Robert Galloway of Edinburgh.[335]

Besides these unspectacular activities for a skipper of Crail, we find him as a long-distance mariner. In 1567, he made a voyage from Crail to Königsberg.[336] Again in 1578 he made a voyage to the Baltic, carrying Scottish salt from Crail to Danzig, where he loaded rye, flour, flax, Swedish iron and ashes.[337]

Also in 1580 he sailed to the Baltic; coming from Crail in ballast, he passed Elsinore outwards on 16 May, and on 21 June he arrived there again on his way back from Danzig with flax, tar and pitch.[338] Both in this year and in 1578 the value of his return cargo from Danzig by far exceeded that of his Scottish goods, which was usual for Scottish trade with the Baltic.[339] In 1581 it was different; from Scotland he carried a cargo of various skins and textiles of which he sold some at Elsinore, where he cleared on 8 July. At his destination Danzig, he loaded iron, flax, ashes, soap, and naval stores, which he cleared at Elsinore on 5 September. The value of his Scottish goods was reckoned as 794 daler, his Baltic goods were estimated at 743 daler.[340] Again in 1587 he left Crail bound for the Baltic with train-oil and herring, skins, blue cloth and kerseys and returned from Königsberg with rye, flax and ropes.[341]

In the course of Thomas Martin's year there would be ample room for other ventures to England, France, the Low Countries or Norway, but here our sources are silent. He must, however, have been a man of a certain standing, as in 1583 he was one of Crail's bailies.[342]

That for a skipper of the East Neuk there was no practical limit between fishing and shipping is seen from the mentioned examples and proven by a contract from 1577. John Spens of Crail obliged himself to furnish by Christmas one last of Northern Scottish herring to John Lindsay of Cupar. If, however, the vessel (a crear) continued to France and sold its cargo there, Spens was to pay to Lindsay the amount for which his herring had been sold.[343] Similarly, skipper John Davidson, whom we find as a contractor in 1572 and again in 1582-3, engaged in fishing as well as in shipping as a carrier of flour and coal.[344]

The ships, often crears, could be used for fishing off the Scottish coast, but were substantitial enough to sail to Norway or France if necessary. Another precondition for the Scottish mariners' flexibility is to be found in their long apprenticeship. During these years the young man would accompany his master on all his voyages, both abroad as a carrier or as a fisherman in Scottish waters. An apprentice taught by a skipper of the East Neuk would have acquired a good knowledge of the North Sea, the Channel and the west coast of France, of the Danish belts and the Baltic as well as of the fishing grounds; on top of that the apprentice would have been initiated to the conditions of trade in these regions.[345]

Thus as far as the contractors were concerned we find a great flexibility. Their ships and their education allowed them to engage in shipping or fishing according to the possibilities of profit. For the contractors, fishing was never a full time occupation, which it could have been for the fishermen in the crew.

## The coopers; mariner contractors or merchants?

Some of the coopers of Crail showed a remarkable flexibility. Sometimes they organized voyages to Norway in order to buy the necessary wood, but as a rule they formed a partnership with a skipper. David Currour appears to have been an exception, as he could conduct a ship and for that reason had been engaged by Andrew Peirson as a skipper.[346] Twice in 1574 he entered goods from Norway, but only his name and the customs paid are given.[347] In 1575 he appears to have imported

Norwegian goods again, but also here only his name and the amount paid are mentioned.[348] Once more, in 1576, David Currour sailed to Norway to fetch timber, for this venture chartering a ship belonging to skipper John Gardiner of Anstruther.[349] Currour again exported to Norway, probably in 1577, six barrels of salt and two barrels of malt, but we do not know what goods he brought home.[350]

Another cooper of Crail, John Morton, also organized voyages for timber, probably always to Norway. In 1568 he was in partnership with John Balfour to whom he owed £15 to be paid by 15 August.[351] In 1569 he traded again with Norway, his part of the freight of Thomas Davidson's vessel to Norway amounting to £14.[352]

In 1571 Morton borrowed £50 from John Melville planning two voyages to Norway in the course of the spring or summer. To this end Morton had chartered a ship, the *Marie Anne*, and agreed to allow Melville to provide a quarter of the cargo. Morton planned to sail to Norway himself, in all likelihood in order to buy the wood. In the first voyage Morton worked again with Thomas Davidson, who was to provide Morton with half the cargo, for which the latter had paid.[353] As the *Marie Anne* belonged to George Peirson and Andro Balcony, Thomas Davidson could have been engaged as the skipper.[354] For the second voyage Morton appears to have chartered William Arnot's vessel.[355] Once again, in 1572, Morton sailed to Norway for wood.[356]

It was only natural that the coopers who imported their wood from Norway should themselves engage in the timber trade. John Morton sold 143 pieces of 'knappet', ie knapholt = clapboard or oak wood used for cask staves, to David Currour,[357] and the latter cooper had obliged himself to provide Patrick Lindsay with 14 'aiken ruiffe spairs' (oaken roof spars), for which Lindsay had lent him £28-8. If Currour were unable to deliver them, he would have to pay Lindsay £56 and at a later date furnish him with ten lasts of herring barrels.[358] To William Annand, Currour obliged himself to deliver five dozen fir deals by 11 November 1578; probably Currour planned a voyage to Norway before the end of the sailing season.[359] Apparently, it was only when John Morton gave up his voyages to Norway that he was admitted as a burgess of Crail;[360] it is very probable that William Morton, cooper, was his son who continued his trade. In 1581 William Morton bought 'knappis' (wooden vats, eg for milk) from Mr John Harte at the Canongate.[361] Also it is likely that David Currour's trade was continued by a son or another relative; in 1589, we read that a certain William Currour had provided James Lauder with barrel hoops and other kinds of wood. [362]

James Lauder and John Myrton were coopers who formed a partnership with skipper John Martin, and in April 1590 they planned a voyage to Norway, for which William Hunter of Crail had advanced them an unspecified working capital; in return they were to provide him with 100 deals by 1 August 1590.[363] Moreover, the three partners obliged themselves to furnish to Alan Cunningham 50 deals by 1 August, further, the two coopers promised to provide him with five lasts of herring barrels, again by 1 August or in time for the autumn fishing.[364] Also John Myrton obliged himself to furnish to John Partie three lasts of herring barrels by 8 September.[365] In November 1590 Myrton was still in debt to Alan Cunningham, to whom Myrton had sold deals and barrels as well as a barrel of herring; moreover, Cunningham had stood surety for Myrton's debt to James Lyall. It is not quite clear, whether Myrton had contracted this debt to Cunningham as his part of the partners' obligations, or if it originated in an independent contract. At any rate, the Burgh Court found that Myrton must either deliver the promised goods to Cunningham or pay him.[366]

Skipper John Martin also engaged in the timber trade outside the partnership with the two coopers. In 1589 he bought barrels and 'skenis treeis' from Robert Arnot, to whom he was to deliver a thousand poles. In this he partly failed and had thus to pay the equivalent of the highest market price.[367]

A few coopers appear to have taken part in the fishing. In November 1567, Robert Mur was at Loch Broom,[368] and in April 1580, William Smyth, cooper, promised to deliver by Christmas to William Morton, cooper, two barrels of herring from Northern Scotland and by 8 September ten lasts of herring barrels, for which Morton was to give him the necessary materials.[369] Again in 1581, Smyth should provide Morton with a barrel of herring.[370]

In 1577, William Currour engaged in the herring fishing, promising to provide David Page at Cupar with a last of herring from Northern Scotland and Patrick Lindsay of Crail with nine barrels, also from Northern Scotland, in each case to be delivered by Christmas.[371]

In spite of his designation as a cooper, William Morton was deeply engaged in fishing. In certain years this was perhaps his main activity. We read that in 1581 he bought wooden vats from Mr John Harte at the Canongate; the year before he had commissioned ten lasts of herring barrels (with two barrels of herring) from William Smyth, cooper, and ten more lasts of herring barrels with one barrel of herring from Robert Morris.[372]

With three more burgesses of Crail William Morton had sold herring to James Dalyell of Edinburgh;[373] and in 1577 he had advanced £31 to Robert Ottar, who by Christmas should deliver him a last of herring from Northern Scotland or, in case of failure, to pay the highest market price. James Corstorphine had received no working capital, but agreed to provide Morton with a last of herring from Northern Scotland on the same conditions.[374] With George Peirson as a surety, Alexander Woed promised to bring Morton by Christmas 18 barrels of herring from Northern Scotland or to pay back the unspecified amount received; John Ottar similarly obliged himself to provide Morton with a last of herring from Northern Scotland by Christmas or to pay the highest market price, and on the same conditions William Daw promised to give to Morton half a last of herring from Northern Scotland.[375]

In 1580 Morton lent John Balcony £80, thus financing part of the latter's fishing; besides this sum Balcony owed Morton a last of herring from Northern Scotland by Christmas. Further, for delivery at the same term Thomas Blair promised Morton two lasts of herring from Northern Scotland, Alexander Kynnaird one last, and Thomas Blair in partnership with John Corstorphine younger also one last.[376]

The dates of the contracts reveal that Morton's engagement referred to the autumn fishing in 1577 as well as in 1580. When in March 1580/1 Arthur Gray promised him a last of herring from Northern Scotland by Christmas 1581, he was free to catch it in the spring or in the autumn.[377] In September 1581, John Martin of Crail promised Morton a last of Northern Scottish herring by Christmas, whereas between them Alexander Kynnaird, John Bruce and Robert Alexander should give him 17 barrels of herring from Northern Scotland at the same term.[378] At the end of December Alexander Kynnaird obliged himself to provide Morton with a last of herring from Northern Scotland by Christmas 1582 or to pay the highest market price. Kynnaird would thus be free to get his herring in the spring or in the autumn. On similar conditions Androw and John Annand promised Morton seven barrels and Arthur Gray one last of herring from Northern Scotland; also John Balcony got a delay to Christmas 1582 for his last of herring from Northern Scotland, but apparently was not to pay the highest market price in case of failure.[379]

To John Wilson, 'huikmaker' (anchorsmith), and Edward Abay, seaman, Morton had advanced unspecified amounts of money, for which they should furnish him respectively half a last and a last of herring from the 'Isles' by Christmas or pay him the highest market price.[380] Also John Balcony promised Morton one last and a half of herring from Northern Scotland (with £4) by Christmas or to pay him the highest market price.[381]

A few of the coopers of Crail imported their wood from Norway and accepted commissions for other kinds of timber. Some of them engaged in fishing, but only William Morton to any great extent. In certain years he should be seen as a merchant rather than as a craftsman. He either bought his barrels from others or put them out to other coopers, eventually furnishing the necessary materials. Morton also commissioned a certain amount of herring and sometimes advanced a working capital to the contractors. In this way he controlled two phases of the production of herring which could give him a larger share of the profit, but our sources do not allow us to see how large it was.

## The merchants

To this group have been assigned both the merchants proper and others who furnished capital to the contractors (ie to the skippers and mariners), and who needed to be paid back some months later in fish. Obviously, the majority came from Crail itself, but some also came from other towns in the region and even from Edinburgh. Table 25 gives an overview of the fishing activities of the more important merchants. If no town of residence is mentioned in the table, the person concerned lived at Crail. In the column 'Customs accounts' we find the quantities declared at Crail according to the customs accounts, whereas the column 'Obligations' gives the quantities agreed upon in the contracts registered in the burgh court books. Sometimes keiling is mentioned instead of herring; keiling is a full-grown or large-sized cod.

Several merchants engaged themselves in the fishing only occasionally, apparently as a supplementary activity in particularly promising years. Robert Findlayson of Dundee had in 1577-1578/9 entered cloth and skins at Dundee and in the following year skins and train-oil.[382] In 1583 he advanced £30 to Alexander Kinnaird and John Edyson, both of Crail. Edyson was to furnish six barrels herring from Northern Scotland and Kinnaird, who in another entry is mentioned as master of the *Angel*, a last of herring from the Isles.[383] In 1584, Findlayson imported a tun of wine from Bordeaux and in 1588 goods from Danzig.[384]

William Hunter, a merchant of Crail, also had business relations with Dundee. He both commissioned herring and fished himself, moreover, he entered 600 schoirlings, 600 lambskins and 200 goatskins in 1578/9-1579/80[385] as well as 11 dozen pieces of cloth in 1582.[386]

Frequently, the merchants commissioned a certain quantity of herring from a contractor, to whom they would advance working capital, while the merchant stayed at home. In the customs accounts the contractors are entered as owners of the load and for that reason we seldom find the merchants themselves in the accounts. If they appear there, we may infer that they had participated more actively in the venture.

### Widows and other female merchants

Sometimes, a widow took over the trade of her husband on his death. In 1566, John Dingwall entered 264 barrels of herring as the result of his fishing;[387] in 1568 he advanced money to two contractors bound for Loch Broom;[388] in 1569 his contractors were bound for Loch Carron or Northern Scotland,[389] while Dingwall himself went to the Baltic with cloth, lambskins and white leather and returned from Königsberg with ashes, pitch, flax and hemp,[390] and in 1570 William Arnot used Dingwall's ship as a contractor for Thomas Welwood of St Andrews.[391] Dingwall must have died in the following year, and in September 1571 his widow Helen Bethell took over. She advanced money to Alexander Laverock and Alexander Woede for a voyage to Northern Scotland and commissioned a last of herring from Laverock.[392] But perhaps the venture had already been agreed upon by John Dingwall before his death; at any rate we do not see Helen Bethell as a merchant any more.

Other widows were active in business on their own account over a longer period; in 1572 Patrick Geddes had advanced £11 to John Smith, part-owner of the *Mary James* for a voyage to Northern Scotland,[393] and in both 1576 and 1577 his widow Margaret Cornwall commissioned herring from Arthur Gray and in 1576 also from John Arrock.[394] Apparently, she took advantage of the promising herring years in 1576-7.

Christine Oliphant also worked as a merchant in her own right in 1581-2,[395] but we do not know whether or not her husband John Cruyk had died when she engaged in the fishing.[396] On the other hand,

Janet Young, William Lumsden's widow, did not participate in the fishing during her husband's lifetime; though in 1590 she commissioned smaller quantities of herring (six barrels each) from three contractors;[397] obviously she wanted to spread the risk. Each contract stipulated that if only two thirds of the agreed quantity could be had, Janet Young was to receive these two thirds, and one third of the advanced sum should be paid back. We find the same clause in the contracts concluded by James Sydserf of Edinburgh in the same year. [398]

### Price and engagement

As one could expect, the merchants would sometimes reckon the value of a last of herring at the same price within the same year. In all of his four contracts from 1574 Nicol Uddart of Edinburgh reckoned the value of a last of herring at £32,[399] and this value was retained in William Melville's four contracts two years later.[400]

In contracts by other merchants we find different values within the same year. In the nine contracts concluded by James Sydserf of Edinburgh in September 1590, the last of herring was once reckoned as £40, four times as £44 and four times as £45.[401] Besides the estimated value of the herring Sydserf had in two cases advanced £20 which was to be paid back with the fish.[402] No allusion in the entries allows us to discover the reason for these differences.

Not all merchants engaged in financing the fishing itself, which was probably the case of Andro Kay of St Andrews. In March 1580 John Eldis (?) of Crail obliged himself to deliver to Kay by 8 September, £23 and one dozen dry fish,[403] and one year later, John Eldis and Alexander Kinnaird recognised a debt of £69 to Andro Kay, who had also furnished them with one dozen dry fish (ling and keiling) to be paid by 15 August.[404] In the latter case, Kay must have provided Eldis and Kinnaird with working capital plus part of the victuals for a voyage, but probably intending trade rather than fishing. The same might be true in 1580, but with the difference that Eldis should fetch dry fish for Kay.

Some merchants advanced money to mariners without themselves engaging either in trade or in fishing. One such was Patrick Geddes in 1572. In 1569 Ninian Hamilton lent Andro Daw younger and Giles Brown £48 in view of a voyage to Loch Carron or Northern Scotland [405] as well as £60 to James Dawson, who obliged himself to pay Hamilton £5 for each voyage.[406] Apparently, Hamilton owned at least part of a ship which Dawson could use for his ventures.

In the 1570s Thomas Kay was active in fishing on his own account: he landed herring from the Forth and elsewhere, as well as 'pale fish' (fish of inferior size) and train-oil. Several times he imported English goods, so in all likelihood he sold his fish south of the Border. From John Hudson of York he had bought corn, for which he did not pay in time. The amount of his debt, £120 Sterling, shows us that it must have been a considerable quantity.[407] In 1569 he and Alexander Airth commissioned a last of herring from Loch Carron or Northern Scotland from Alexander Farmer and at the same time Kay advanced £12 to George Davidson in view of his voyage to Loch Carron or Northern Scotland.[408] Probably the obligations refer to the same venture.

## Patrick Lindsay, a *socius stans*[409]

Patrick Lindsay may be considered a *socius stans*, the senior investor in a partnership who stayed at home, as opposed to a *socius itinerans* who travelled with the ship. Jointly with Alexander Ramsay, in 1566/7 he arranged to land 12 lasts of herring, and in the 1570s he did not fish himself but regularly commissioned moderate quantities of fish, from various contractors in order to spread the risk. David Currour, cooper, owed him £27 and obliged himself to deliver seven herring barrels within four weeks.[410] In September 1571, he lent Thomas Davidson, skipper, £36 to be paid by Christmas; probably Lindsay had advanced him working capital for the coming venture.[411] Some days earlier, Lindsay advanced £13 to Alexander Woede, who obliged himself to deliver six barrels of herring to Lindsay by Christmas. At the same time, Lindsay lent William Daw £20-8, of which £8-10 should be paid back by Christmas. As on the same day Daw recognised his debt of £24 to be paid by Christmas to John Cruyk,[412] Daw could have been the skipper who organised the voyage.

In 1572, Lindsay again commissioned herring from various contractors, among these Andro Baxter, who promised to deliver by Christmas a last of herring from Northern Scotland; Lindsay had advanced two sums, £24 and £12,[413] which could have been part of the venture's working capital. Two days later George Peirson promised to give Patrick Lindsay a quarter of his expected cargo from Northern Scotland ('...off quhatsumeuer guids gair quhilk he sal happen to gett in the northern partis off this realme...'). Moreover, Lindsay had advanced a quarter of the sum, which Alexander Woede owed for his part, probably of the cargo. The latter recognised himself debtor to Lindsay for £96-14 Scots to be paid by Christmas.[414]

Also in 1573, Lindsay commissioned herring from various other contractors, but it remains unclear why the amounts advanced were so different. Robert Arrock and Andro Baxter each obliged themselves to deliver to Lindsay by Christmas a last of herring from Northern Scotland, but Arrock had received £35 and Baxter only £12.[415] Some days later Nicol John of Anstruther recognized his debt of £24 to Lindsay and David Scott obliged himself to deliver to him by Christmas a barrel of herring.[416] Apparently Nicol John was the mariner who organized the venture and Scott one of the other contractors.

Thus Patrick Lindsay financed some of these ventures, in part, thereby limiting the risk to his investment. When in 1576 he did not participate actively in the fishing itself, he nevertheless ordered 13 lasts of herring barrels from David Currour to be delivered by 1 August; probably he would make them available to the mariners of the autumn fishing.[417]

Besides his moderate engagement in financing active fishing, Lindsay was to a certain extent a general purveyor of capital for the venturers. Other entries in the burgh court books mention individual obligations to him, but it is seldom possible to see to what purpose the debt had been contracted. As a merchant Lindsay was prudent, spreading the risk and never engaging himself too much in a single venture.[418] Moderate quantities of herring were commissioned every year, as a rule between three and four lasts, though in 1577 the experience of the excellent herring year in 1576 must have convinced him of the merits of commissioning a larger quantity. The herring trade was thus one of his activities, perhaps on a rather local level, but money-lending more widely was another and perhaps more important interest.

### Walter Ballingall, investor in herring and herring barrels

Like Lindsay, other merchants ordered herring barrels from the coopers. Walter Ballingall was one of these; he also apparently did not fish himself, but regularly commissioned moderate quantities of herring. The fishing had been good in 1576, and in the autumn of that year he commissioned from David Arrock two lasts of herring barrels to be delivered by 15 January 1576/7.[419] The amount advanced, £46-13-4, considerably exceeds the value of the barrels and must have included money for another purpose. If Arrock participated in David Currour's voyage to Norway (see the preceding section) in order to fetch timber, the surplus could have been intended as a working capital, but this must remain pure speculation.

Currour was back in Scotland in December, and in January he obliged himself to deliver to Ballingall by 15 August 1577 twelve and a half lasts of herring barrels.[420] This quantity greatly exceeded the number of barrels commissioned by Ballingall at the start of 1577, he probably then sold them on to the mariners preparing a venture. The term of delivery agreed would put the barrels at his disposal in time for the autumn fishing.

**William Annand, the occasional fisherman and David Currour's customer and *socius stans***

With the exception of the years 1569-1571, William Annand did not himself engage regularly in the fishing, though in 1576, 1577-1578/9 and perhaps also in 1580,[421] he fished actively on his own behalf. In 1576 he commissioned a barrel of train-oil from William Hawson to be delivered by 15 August,[422] and after the autumn fishing he commissioned herring barrels from David Currour, two lasts by 8 January 1576/7 and 10 lasts by 15 August 1577. In May Currour still owed Annand £9-5-0, which could mean that he had not completely honoured his obligation.[423]

In August of the following year, Currour obliged himself to deliver to Annand two lasts of herring barrels within two weeks: obviously Annand wanted to receive them in time for the autumn fishing. Moreover, Annand had furnished him with 20 barrels small (ie Scottish) salt at a value of £15 to be paid by 11 November or to prepare for him by Christmas five lasts of herring barrels by Christmas. Finally, Annand expected to receive by Martinmas (11 November) five dozen fir deals ('fyrue dailes').[424] As salt was one of the staple goods exported to Norway, Currour was obviously preparing a voyage across the North Sea in the autumn in order to fetch timber.

**Alan Cunningham, dealer in herring barrels**

We can only partly reconstruct Alan Cunningham's activities. In the middle of the 1570s, he declared train-oil and salt to the customs authorities and commissioned fairly large quantities of herring in 1582 and 1583. In 1578, George Davidson owed him £32 and a last of herring barrels to be delivered by 15 August.[425]

Like other merchants, Cunningham put herring barrels at the disposal of mariners: in April 1583 Robert King younger, cooper, obliged himself to deliver to Cunningham by 26 May, £20 which he had borrowed from Cunningham, and six new herring barrels. If he could not pay, he was to furnish Cunningham with seven and a half lasts of herring barrels by 15 August , in time for the autumn fishing.[426]

Later in the same year, Cunningham made a venture with Robert Alexander, seaman, who was bound for Northern Scotland. It was the classic partnership, in which one partner, usually the elder, stayed at home (*socius stans*), whereas the other (*socius itinerans*) travelled. At his own expense Cunningham was to charter a vessel, the *Jo,* for herring fishing off Northern Scotland. When Alexander returned, Cunningham was to furnish salt, barrels and part of the props used to support the vessel on land. In return Alexander should give Cunningham half his catch of fish and on top of that one barrel fish per last.[427]

We do not know Cunningham's activities for the next years, but in 1590 he commissioned herring barrels from John Myrton, cooper, who also sold him timber (see preceding section). The letting or sale of herring barrrels must have been one of Cunningham's main activities.

**The two John Melvilles**

The two merchants, both called John Melville, are problematic. In 1579 'John Melville younger' appears in one entry, but in the next, in 1581, only 'John Melville' is mentioned, without qualification. We meet the name John Melville for the first time in 1570, so he was the elder of the two; he was still living in 1579, when the scribe of the burgh court book found it necessary to distinguish the two burgesses of the same name from each other. One of them must have died by 1581, as from that year on, once again, only one John Melville is mentioned. Full certainty cannot be obtained, but it can be assumed that the survivor was John Melville younger. This man began his career in 1579 as contractor for Andrew Melville younger of Anstruther, a possible relative, to whom he was to deliver a last of herring from Northern Scotland by 1 January 1579/80.[428] In 1581/2 and 1590 he worked mainly as a merchant, commissioning various quantities of herring from several contractors.

In an agreement of 30 April 1582 he appears as a contractor. Robert Blackburn, citizen of Rouen in France, had asked his brother John Blackburn younger of Edinburgh to procure him four and a half lasts of Scottish herring to be delivered in two equal instalments by 2 February 1582/3 and 1583/4. With William Morton as a surety, John Melville obliged himself to furnish the herring as described. On the other side, William Bowsie of Crail stood surety for John Blackburn's payment of 400 francs on his brother's behalf to John Melville, who obliged himself to issue a receipt when he had received the money.[429] Strictly speaking, Melville was the contractor, but the complexity and the international connection of the transaction place him at the level of a merchant.

Let us return to John Melville elder, whom we meet for the first time in 1570 when he, as a contractor, obliged himself to furnish to John Wemyss of Edinburgh a last of herring from Northern Scotland by 10 January 1570/1. Further, he had lent Robert Morton £8 and advanced to the latter's brother, John Morton, cooper, £44 in return for two lasts of herring barrels and half a last of puncheons; the brothers were to pay their respective debts by 30 November 1570.[430]

In 1571, he participated in John Morton's venture to Norway,[431] but Melville still owed part of the charter of the *Marie Anne* to George Peirson and Andro Balcony from an earlier voyage whose destination we do not know. Moreover, Melville had commissioned from Alexander Shorting a last of herring to be delivered by Marymas (15 August).[432] Later in the year, Melville lent Morton £80 to be paid in two instalments by 8 September 1572 and 1573, Morton guaranteeing Melville the delivery of 18 barrels.[433] In all likelihood, Melville advanced working capital for the coming two ventures, and we know that at least in 1572 Morton sailed to Norway for timber.

In 1573 Melville commissioned herring from Alexander Farmer who was to get it from two different ships, and in the winter of 1573-4 he ordered three lasts of herring barrels from Alexander Stobhill at Kilrennie ('Kylrynnie') to be delivered by 8 August, thus in time for the autumn fishing.[434] Perhaps in 1574, he landed 18 barrels, probably of herring,[435] and in 1575, 210 barrels of Forth herring and 228 barrels of packed keiling.[436] Probably in 1577, he exported 10 barrels of salt with two dozen pieces of cloth to Norway,[437] where presumably he also bought timber. In 1578 he commissioned herring from Loch Broom, which Andro Melville of Anstruther had furnished, but for which John Melville only partly paid.[438]

**Outside merchants**

The large majority of merchants mentioned in the burgh court books were established at Crail, but a few lived in other burghs on the Firth of Forth. In addition, we have already met Robert Blackburn of Rouen, and in 1569, the Englishman Robert Constable commissioned herring from contractors of Crail.[439] These two were, however, the only foreign merchants involved in the fisheries of Crail.

Some of the outside Scottish merchants were active in only one year, like George Christie of Dysart, who in 1569 commissioned herring from three different contractors.[440] Robert Findlayson of Dundee we have also met already, but in view of the close contacts in shipping between Dundee and the East Neuk it is surprising to find only one more merchant of Dundee, John Traille, who engaged in Crail's fisheries, and then only with small quantities, in 1581 and 1582. In 1578/9-1579/80 he entered hides and cloth at Dundee.[441] He was admitted a burgess of Dundee on 2 March 1570/1[442] and must 10 years later have been one of the established merchants. Herring fishing must have been one of his minor activities.

From Crail's neighbour towns we know of rather few merchants. William Powsta of Cellardyke commissioned small quantities, mainly of dry fish, in 1574 and 1590,[443] whereas Andro Melville of Anstruther was active in the middle of the 1570s in the Forth fishing as well as in trade with England; later in 1579, he commissioned a last of herring.[444] At St Andrews, Andro Kay appears to have furnished victuals to other ships as we have seen; about 1580, Archibald Wishart commissioned smaller quantities of herring from contractors at Crail, and in September 1589 one and a half lasts of Loch Broom herring from Andrew Davidson, skipper of St Andrews, who had received £63 in advance.[445] In the 1580s, John[446] and Thomas Welwood commissioned modest quantities of herring, but in 1582-3 Thomas must have taken a more active part in the fishing.[447]

From burghs somewhat further away, we find Patrick Hogg of Kirkcaldy, who in the good years in the middle 1570s and again in 1580 commissioned herring from various contractors.[448] In 1576 and 1577 he worked with John Dawson, but in the latter year Dawson must have been unable to find the required three lasts of herring from the Isles and had to pay Hogg £135 at £45 per last, no doubt the equivalent of the highest market price. Together with Robert Hay, Hogg imported to Edinburgh English 'stemmyng' (a kind of woollen cloth) in 1589-1590.[449]

On the other side of the Firth of Forth, at Prestonpans, Alexander Reid was active in the fishing in the years 1569-1571. In all three years he commissioned from contractors of Crail various quantities of herring, mainly from Northern Scotland. In 1571 one of his contractors was a certain John Reid, who could have been a relative, and in both 1570 and 1571 Thomas Martin was one of the contractors. Probably fishing was only part of his economic activities in these three years and only in 1570-1 he fished himself.[450]

### The merchants of Edinburgh involved in Crail; Queen's Men and King's Men

The end of Queen Mary's rule divided Scotland into two camps, Queen's Men and King's Men. The documentation from Edinburgh allows us often to know the political affiliation of a person. In respect of Crail, we only know that a group of its inhabitants refused to deliver up certain of the Earl of Bothwell's servants to the authorities and the Privy Council therefore considered them implicated in Bothwell's crimes and ordered them to appear before them. Among them we find Thomas Beane ('Bane'), William Bowsie (probably the elder), William Kay, Robert Arnot, and John Reid.[451] Arnot was frequently mentioned as a contractor, whereas the others appear among those commissioning fish. They must be assumed to have been Queen's Men.

Among the merchants of the capital with business relations to Crail, we find Alexander Arbuthnot, merchant and bookseller. He was mentioned as a Queen's Man in 1571 and died in 1585.[452] One of his business friends at Crail was William Kay, with whom he worked in 1569, and who two years earlier the Privy Council had considered implicated in Bothwell's misdeeds.

John Dougall younger was a merchant of Edinburgh, whom we find among the King's Men in 1572. In 1581, he commissioned herring and he cleared train-oil at Crail in the following year (Table 25). He was considered a radical and thus probably supported the Ruthven regime 1582-3. After its fall, he was exiled from Edinburgh in 1584, but must have been allowed to return shortly afterwards. He was elected a Deacon of the Kirk Session in 1584-5 and died in 1601.[453] As there are two merchants both called John Dougall and as the customs accounts seldom mention whether or not the elder or the younger is meant, it is difficult to get a precise idea of their trading activities (Table 26). Thus the goods cleared by the merchants John Dougall at Edinburgh/Leith were mainly cloth, skins and hides; moreover, they regularly imported English goods.

John MacMorran, merchant, must have belonged to the same party. In 1582 he commissioned herring and at the same time fished himself (Table 25). He was considered a radical and in 1582 had to procure a security for his good conduct. For the year 1584-5 he was elected a Deacon of the Kirk Session and a councillor for 1586-7; in 1596 he died as a rich man.[454] In 1579/80 he entered 45 dozen cloth, 90 daker hides and 30 barrels herring/codling at Edinburgh and had to pay £6 wax (?) money, which could mean that he had imported wax, probably from the Baltic region.[455] In 1589-90 he fetched from Moray, 102 barrels salmon and 140 ells ('elnis') plaiding.[456] In the following year, he entered 18 daker wild leather or harthides, 59 daker ordinary hides, 20 chalders coal, eight polks woad: further he paid, along with Alexander Makmath, £1-5-0 customs for flax and hemp and in company with Ninian MacMorran and Mungo McCall £60 customs for wax and £6 for copper.[457] Apparently, his two partnerships had imported goods from the Baltic region.

Before his death in 1583, Robert Arnot in Crail had received a commission of 25 barrels herring from William Napier of Edinburgh.[458] This wealthy merchant was a King's Man in 1572-3 and one of the bailies in 1574-5. He was a councillor from April to October 1578, a bailie 1580-1 and again a councillor 1581-2. He was an elder of the Kirk in 1573-4 and again in 1584-5.[459] In 1585 he was again elected one of the bailies for 1585-6 and one of the councillors for 1586-7.[460] In May 1585 he was chosen one of the supervisors of the dredging of the 'mwre' and a few days later he was with Nicol Uddart and four other burgesses elected to negotiate over the future of Paisley Abbey.[461] He appears only once to have engaged in Crail's fishing, which obviously does not exclude other mercantile activities. Thus in 1575-6 he entered at Edinburgh 240 skins, one barrel salt and paid £6 wax money.[462] In 1578-9, he entered three barrels and one 'firrikin' of salmon[463] and in 1589-90, 200 'daillis' (deals).[464] Thus, occasionally, he appears to have imported goods from abroad, wax from the Baltic region or timber from Norway. However, it is legitimate to ask, if his numerous political charges would have left him much time for business.

The same holds true for another wealthy merchant, Nicol Uddart. He was mentioned as a 'faithful brother' in 1562, as a councillor in 1562-3, a bailie in 1563-4, and a councillor again in 1566-7. From October 1570 to June 1571 and again in 1572-3 he was Treasurer of the burgh; in 1574-5 he was a bailie and in the following year a councillor for the third time, and for the fourth time in 1586-7. In

1570 he was considered to be one of the King's Men, which caused his house to be demolished by the Queen's party in the spring of 1572. In 1574-5 he was one of the Kirk Elders. He was elected Dean of Guild in October 1584 and re-elected for another year in 1585.[465]

Besides his commissions of herring from contractors of Crail in 1574, we know that he traded with France in 1571,[466] and in 1573-4 he entered five dozen pieces of cloth and 100 skins.[467] In 1575-6 he declared six dozen pieces of cloth and paid £2 wax money, which could refer to his import of this article from the Baltic region,[468] and in the autumn of 1578 with other merchants and mariners he imported wine from Bordeaux. One year later, as a protest against his tax assessment he resigned from his freedom as a burgess, which the council did not accept.[469]

His business experience was recognised by the town; in December 1574 he was appointed one of the men sent to Dalkeith to negotiate with Regent Morton, about the export of salt and about the coinage.[470] Ten years later he was among those chosen to discuss ecclesiastical affairs with representatives of the Kirk.[471]

We know that he traded with France where there was a market for Scottish herring, which could explain his engagement in the fisheries of Crail. His other mercantile activities we do not know, but again, as with William Napier, one could ask whether or not his political involvement would leave him much time for business.

In the 1580s we find that James and John Summerville, both of Edinburgh, commissioned herring from contractors of Crail, among them Arthur Gray (see first section of this chapter). James Summerville was taxed 50s. in 1583,[472] a modest amount, and in 1580 John Summerville, messenger, was chosen to collect the poor rate.[473] John Summerville does not appear in the customs accounts of Edinburgh/ Leith, but James declared two dozen pieces of cloth and one daker hides in 1575-6,[474] in 1578-9 six daker hides, 10 barrels salmon as well as eight lasts and an unknown number of barrels herring/codling.[475] Moreover, in company with Thomas Paterson he declared nine lasts of herring coming from Anstruther in 1580-1.[476] Clearly, the Somervilles participated exclusively in trade within Scotland.

James Sydserf of Edinburgh commissioned a considerable quantity of herring in 1590 from contractors of Crail. Already in 1579-80 he had declared 123 barrels herring/codling at Edinburgh and paid in 1589-90 £10-2 customs for imported English goods.[477] His numerous contractors at Crail in 1590 reveal that he sought to spread the risk. Regularly, when the merchant had advanced money to the contractor, the agreement stipulated that if only two-thirds of the agreed quantity were to be had, they should be delivered in fish and the last third of the sum paid back in cash.

Among the Edinburgh merchants engaged in Crail's fishing we find John Wemyss, who in 1570 commissioned two lasts of herring, one from William Kay and one from John Melville. The former was among the men whom the Privy Council had considered implicated in Bothwell's deeds, and Wemyss appears among the Queen's Men.[478] In 1579/80 he declared 12 lasts of herring/codling at Edinburgh.[479] Obviously, he only occasionally engaged himself in the herring trade.

More can be said about Mister John Harte of the Canongate. In 1576, 1578 and 1580-2 he commissioned various quantities of herring from contractors of Crail. More than once he worked with Robert Arnot and Arthur Gray, but otherwise he tried to spread the risk by using various contractors. Although topographically part of the Edinburgh conurbation, legally speaking the Canongate was an independent burgh with its own jurisdiction. Mister John Harte, son of John Harte,[480] was mentioned as a bailie of the Canongate in December 1579, November 1580 and October 1581.[481] We know of his engagements in the fisheries of Crail, and also that with John Arnot he actively participated in the fishing. In 1579-80 he paid £6 customs on goods imported from England:[482] perhaps he had sold some of his herring south of the border to pay for his imports.

The burgh court books of the Canongate add further information on his interests in the fisheries. In September 1575 David Smeton of the Canongate acknowledged having received from Harte £52; in return he obliged himself to deliver by 11 November two lasts of herring from Loch Broom or to pay the equivalent of the highest market price.[483] Smeton could not deliver the herring agreed upon, and on 6 June 1577 the Burgh Court decided that he should pay the highest market price or £50 per last.[484] In June 1578, John Seyton of the Canongate acknowledged a debt to Harte of £92, in return for which he should deliver at Leith four lasts of Dunbar herring by 8 September ('Latter Lady day of Harvist') or to pay the equivalent of the highest market price by 11 November.[485]

In March 1582/3 Harte stood surety for William Bowsie of Crail, who owed to James Summerville £30 to be paid by Christmas 1583. The yearly interest was five merks to be paid in two instalments, at Whitsuntide and on 11 November. If the £30 were the whole capital, the rate of interest would be 11.1 %. Apparently the transaction concerned the rent of a tenement and yard at Crail belonging to Robert King.[486]

Harte's activities show him as a merchant for whom herring was a main article. Consequently, he tried to procure it from various sources – Dunbar, Loch Broom and the regions visited by the mariners of Crail, mainly Northern Scotland. Where he sold his herring, in Scotland or abroad, we do not know.

# Conclusions

The investigation made it possible to see the organisation of the fisheries, not as the statutes and decrees intended them to be, but as they actually were. As a source, the importance of the burgh court books of Crail cannot be exaggerated: digitalisation of the eight surviving volumes would allow us to discover so many aspects of daily life in this small Scottish town that it could almost be compared to Montaillou at the foot of the Pyrenees, where an equally full documentation allowed Emmanuel Le Roy Ladurie to write one of the classics of medieval social history. [487]

In chapter one the technical preconditions for the fishing were dealt with. The difficulty in finding convenient timber in Scotland caused some coopers to travel to Norway for timber, and also certain merchants specialised in the trade in herring barrels. Salt for preserving the fish was produced in Scotland and was often used for curing Scottish herring. However, imported salt was better and guaranteed a higher quality of the herring. It mainly came from Western France, where Scottish ships would call in late autumn, not only for salt, but also for the new wine. Finally, the necessary equipment (nets, lines, hooks, etc) was described.

Chapter two identified the fishing grounds and their seasons; by calling at different places, a full-time mariner would be able to fish almost all year round. The main fishing grounds were the Northern Isles, especially Shetland, where a considerable exchange of goods also took place, Loch Broom, Loch Carron, the Isles (ie the Hebrides), Northern Scotland and the Firth of Forth. Loch Broom and Loch Carron are mentioned only in some years, which does not mean that they were not visited in other years. It is probable that the contracts found it more reasonable to specify 'Northern Scotland', which would allow the contractors to fish somewhere else if the herring stayed away from Loch Broom or Loch Carron.

Chapter three dealt with the different types of fish (mainly herring) caught by Crail's fishermen. Sometimes, the furnisher of capital would accept other kinds of fish than herring, mainly keiling (ie full size cod). The latter were caught on handlines, whereas herring were taken in a net.

Famous for their role in the herring fishing are the Dutch buss, where the herring were prepared on board. Given the distance between Crail and the fishing grounds, the fish caught by the Scottish boats must also have undergone at least a provisional cure, while at Crail the final packing would have taken place. Herring caught in the Forth itself would have been entirely processed locally on shore.

This chapter also included an attempt to calculate the quantities caught. For several reasons the figures must be considered as minima: the obligations mention only the quantities which the contractors had to deliver, and the contracts would above all refer to fishing far away, not to the fishing in the Firth of Forth. The latter, however, in so far as they concern exports, we find reflected in the Customs Accounts, but these have survived for only a few years, and, besides, the collection of customs was farmed out for certain periods.[488] Further, the extent of fraud (false or missing declarations) can hardly be gauged. One might also have expected that large quantities would have been declared at Dundee or Edinburgh/Leith, but this happened less often than one would have thought.

Chapter four discussed the economic aspects of the fisheries. The contracts give us the estimated value of a last of herring (the amount of money advanced and the quantity of herring to be delivered); thus, if we can estimate the cost of production of a last of herring, the gross profit can be calculated. Among the production costs one must consider the cost of barrels, of salt, the charter of a ship and the cost of victuals for the crew. The type of vessel used was often a crear, and the size of this vessel and its loading capacity are discussed. To these fitting-out expenses must be added customs and other duties. The comparison of the production costs with the value of a last of herring shows that the profits were always more than 100 %, in two of the six years even over 200%.

Much herring was exported, probably above all to England and France. Smaller quantities entered the Baltic and their value is given in the Danish Sound Toll Registers. In this way it is possible to calculate the added value or profit between the local furnisher of capital and the export merchant: for the three years possible to calculate, the profit was between 41% and 69%.

A specific section of this chapter dealt with the interest charged by the furnishers of capital and the indemnities received, if no fish was to be had.

Chapter five introduced the persons engaged in the fisheries, beginning with the mariner contractors who sailed the crears to the north. For them, fishing was not a full-time activity, but was undertaken only in certain years. Several contractors must have sailed directly to England and elsewhere with part of their catch, but Norway was also an important trading partner. Salt and cloth from Scotland were exchanged for Norwegian timber. For a skipper of the East Neuk there was no practical limit between fishing and shipping; his long apprenticeship had prepared him for both. This flexibility as far as shipping is concerned is characteristic of Scottish mariners: in the later 17th century Scots engaged regularly in tramping within the Baltic region.[489]

The coopers form a particular group; sometimes they were contractors who engaged to furnish a certain quantity of barrels to the merchants, sometimes they took part in trade as merchants, when they fetched timber in Norway or even engaged in fishing themselves.

Generally, the merchants financed the fishing through their commissions, but normally they would not sail themselves, but remained at home. Several types of merchants can be distinguished. There were female merchants, often widows of mariners. There was the furnisher of capital who did not sail himself and as a circumspect merchant tried to spread the risk, and whose main activity was money-lending. We also find the merchant who traded mainly in herring barrels, as well as merchants from other towns who engaged in Crail's fisheries. Those of Edinburgh are especially interesting, because the capital's rich documentation gives us an impression of not only their economic, but also their political, interests. One of these merchants evidently specialised in herring, which he got not only from contractors of Crail, but also those of his own burgh of the Canongate. Some of them took part in international trade, but for most of them their role in internal Scottish trade was more important. From the zones of production in the countryside they brought cloth, skins and hides into the towns, and their engagement in the fisheries could also be seen as part of the process of channelling Scottish products from the rural districts into the burghs.

# Notes

1   This research was made possible by the Carlsberg Foundation of Copenhagen that financed my research fellowship in the Department of Scottish History, University of St Andrews. My work was supervised by Professors T C Smout, St Andrews, and the late Kristof Glamann, Copenhagen; its results were published in 1988: Riis T *Should Auld Acquaintance Be Forgot...Scottish – Danish relations c. 1450-1707*, 2 vols (1988, Odense: Odense University Press).

2   Barrett, J H, Nicholson, R A and Cerón-Carrasco, R, 'Archaeo-ichtyological Evidence for Longterm Socioeconomic Trends in Northern Scotland: 3500 BC to AD 1500', *Journal of Archaeological Science* 26, (1999), pp 360, 365-6 and 369-70.

3   Tracy, J D, 'Herring Wars: the Habsburg Netherlands and the Struggle for Control of the North Sea, ca. 1520-1560', *Sixteenth Century Journal* 24, (1993), p. 252.

4   Smylie, M, *Herring. A History of the Silver Darlings*, 2nd ed., (2011, Brinscombe Port: Stroud), p. 53.

5    Coull, J R, *The Sea Fisheries of Scotland. A Historical Geography*, (1996,Edinburgh: John Donald), p. 54.

6   Unger, R W, 'Dutch Herring, Technology and International Trade in the Seventeenth Century', *Journal of Economic History* 40, (1980), pp. 253 and 263.

7   Ibid., pp. 255 and 258.

8   Tracy, 'Herring Wars', pp 252-3 and 255. In the Shetland fishing the 'buss' were accompanied by the auxiliary ships, the so-called jaggers, which took the herring caught between June 24th and July 15th to Holland, Hamburg or Bremen, see Fenton, A, *The Northern Isles: Orkney and Shetland*, (1978, Edinburgh: Donald), p. 604.

9   Michell, A R, 'The European Fisheries in Early Modern History', in Rich, E E, and Wilson, C (eds), *The Cambridge Economic History of Europe* V, (1987, Cambridge: Cambridge University Press), p. 142.

10  Ibid, pp. 142-3 and 154.

11  van Bochove, C , 'The 'Golden Mountain': An Economic Analysis of Holland's Early Modern Herring Fisheries', in Sicking, L and Abreu-Ferreira, D (eds) *Beyond the Catch: Fisheries of the North Atlantic, the North Sea and the Baltic, 900-1850,* (2009, Leiden-Boston : Brill), pp. 212 and 220-1.

[12]  Ibid, p. 212; Unger, 'Dutch Herring', pp. 259-60; Gibson, W M, *The Herring Fishing I: Stronsay*, (1984, Edinburgh: B.P.P.), p. 43.

[13]  Sicking, L, 'Protection Costs and Profitability of the Herring Fishery in the Netherlands in the Sixteenth Century: A Case Study', *International Journal of Maritime History* 15,2, (2003), p. 269.

[14]  Coull, J R, 'The Development of Herring Fishing in the Outer Hebrides', *International Journal of Maritime History* 15,2, (2003), p. 26.

[15]  van Bochove, 'The 'Golden Mountain'', p. 211; Poulsen, B, *Dutch Herring. An Environmental History, c. 1600-1860*, (2008, Amsterdam: Uitgeverij Aksant), pp. 44 and 208.

[16]  Coull, J R, Fenton, A and Veitch, K (eds), *Boats, Fishing and the Sea: Scottish Life and Society: A Compendium of Scottish Ethnology* IV, (2008, Edinburgh: John Donald in association with The European Ethnological Research Centre), pp. 173-4.

[17]  Sutherland, I, *From Herring to Seine Net Fishing on the East Coast of Scotland*, (1985, Wick: Camps Bookshop), pp. 18-9 and 41.

[18]  Rorke, M, 'The Scottish Herring Trade, 1470-1600', *Scottish Historical Review* 84, (2005), pp. 160-1; Coull, *The Sea Fisheries of Scotland*, p. 75. According to A. R. Michell the ports on the Clyde sent their herring mostly to France, the harbours on the Forth mainly to the Baltic, see 'The European Fisheries', pp. 147-8.

[19]  Coull, *The Sea Fisheries of Scotland*, pp. 67-8; Smylie, *Herring*, p. 119.

[20]  Goodlad, C A, *Shetland Fishing Saga*, (1971, Lerwick: Shetland Times Ltd.), p. 25; cf. also Smith, H D, *Shetland Life and Trade 1550-1914*, (1984, Edinburgh: Donald), p. 3. As Smith considers fishermen based in Shetland, the seasonal cycle according to him is slightly different.

[21]  Smith, *Shetland Life and Trade*, pp. 3, 10-1, 13-5, and 17-9; Coull, *The Sea Fisheries of Scotland*, pp. 86-7.

[22]  Guy, I The Scottish Export Trade, 1460-1599, from the Exchequer Rolls, (1982, unpubl M Phil Thesis , University of St Andrews), p. 124.

[23]  Rorke, 'The Scottish Herring Trade', pp. 155 and 161; Coull, *The Sea Fisheries of Scotland*, pp. 65-6.

[24]  Rorke, 'The Scottish Herring Trade', p. 154.

[25]  Guy, I, The Scottish Export Trade, p. 126.

[26]  Das älteste Rostocker Stadtbuch etwa 1254-1273. Mit Beiträgen zur Geschichte Rostocks im 13. Jahrhundert, ed Thierfelder, H, (1967, Göttingen: Vandenhoeck & Ruprecht).

27  Das älteste Wismarsche Stadtbuch von etwa 1250 bis 1272 , ed Techen, F, (1912, Wismar: Hinstorff); Das zweite Wismarsche Stadtbuch 1272-1297. Liber vel de impignoratione vel emptione seu venditione hereditatum vel aliorum bonorum , 2 vols, ed Lotte Knabe unter Mitwirkung von Anneliese Düring (Quellen und Darstellungen zur Hansischen Geschichte NF XIV 1-2), (1966, Weimar: Böhlau).

28  *Das älteste Stralsundische Stadtbuch 1270-1310*, ed Fabricius, K W F, (1872, Berlin: Weber); *Das Zweite Stralsundische Stadtbuch 1310-1342*, 2 vols, eds Reuter, C, Lietz, P and Wehner, O, (1896-1903, Stralsund: Verlag der Königlichen Regierungs-Buchdruckerei); *Der Stralsunder Liber memorialis*, 6 vols, ed Schröder, H-D, (1964-1988, Rostock-Schwerin-Weimar: Böhlau).

29  Cf. Rehme, P, Das Lübecker Ober-Stadtbuch. Ein Beitrag zur Geschichte der Rechtsquellen und des Liegenschaftsrechtes. Mit einem Urkundenbuche, (1895, Hannover: Helwing).

30  NAS B 10/1/1, Protocol Book of Crail 1566/7-1574 and 1641-1652; B 10/1/2, Protocol Book of Crail 1589-1600.

31  See in general Riis, T, *Should Auld Acquaintance Be Forgot*, I chapter 2 and II, pp 29-51 (Crail's Baltic trade).

32  ULStA B 10/8/8, Burgh Court Book of Crail 22 February 1588-9 – 18 February 1591-2, entry of 7 April 1589.

33  ULStA B 10/8/8.

34  NAS E 71/6/1-10.

35  *Die Recesse und andere Akten der Hansetage von 1256-1430* II ed. Koppmann, K (1872,Leipzig: Duncker & Humblot) , nos. 86 § 16 (1375, p 101), cf. 113 § 3 (1376, p 121).

36  Jahnke, C, *Das Silber des Meeres. Fang und Vertrieb von Ostseehering zwischen Norwegen und Italien (12.-16. Jahrhundert)*, Quellen und Darstellungen zur Hansischen Geschichte Neue Folge XLIX, (2000, Köln-Weimar-Wien: Böhlau), p 220.

37  *The Acts of the Parliaments of Scotland* II A.D. MCCCCXXIV- A.D. MDLXVII ed. Thomson, T, (1814, London), p 119 § 9 (1487, after 1 June).

38  Ibid, pp 178-9 § 16 (1487, after 1 October).

39  Ibid, pp 235 § 20 and 237 § 23.

40  Ibid, p 375 § 28 (1540/1, after 14 March).

41  *Records of the Convention of the Royal Burghs of Scotland...*I: 1295-1597, ed. Marwick, J D, (1866, Edinburgh: W. Paterson), p 23. This measure would correspond to *c* 1.36 hl., cf Zupko, R E, 'The Weights and Measures of Scotland before the Union', *Scottish Historical Review* 56, (1977), p 124.

42 *The Acts of the Parliament of Scotland* III A.D. MDLXVII – A.D. MDXCII ed. Thomson, T, (1814, London ), pp 82-3 § 4 (30 April 1573). In 1587 the Stirling pint was defined as two pounds nine ounces troy weight of clear water, ibid., p 521 § 136 (29 July 1587).

43 Zupko, 'Weights and Measures' , pp 124 and 139.

44 Comar, R D, Simpson, A D C and Morrison-Low, A D, *Weights and Measures in Scotland: a European Perspective*, (2004, East Linton: Tuckwell Press), pp 242-3.

45 Verlinden, C ed., Documents pour l'histoire des prix et des salaries en Flandre et en Brabant (XVe-XVIIIe siècle) / Dokumenten voor de Geschiedenis van prijzen en lonen in Vlaanderen en Brabant (XVe-XVIIIe eeuw), (1959, Bruges: De Tempel), p 11.

46 ULStA B 10/8/4, 23 February 1567/8.

47 *A Dictionary of the Older Scottish Tongue…*VI, (1986, Aberdeen: Aberdeen University Press), p 397.

48 ULStA B 10/8/5, 24 and 31 October 1570 (James Monipenny paid in advance David Currour, cooper, for barrels); 19 April 1571 (John Melvyn paid in advance Alexander Shorting for barrels); B 10/8/6 7 April 1576 (Patrick Lindsay paid in advance David Currour, cooper); B 10/8/8 24 November 1590 (Allan Cunningham paid in advance John Myrton, cooper).

49 ULStA B 10/8/6.

50 See e.g. ULStA B 10/8/5, 5 January 1571/2 (David Currour, cooper, and Patrick Lindsay, seven barrels to deliver within 29 days).

51 ULStA B 10/8/2 (15 and 22 February 1556/7) and B 10/8/6 (27 August 1578).

52 Thus on 6 July 1591 the court found that skipper John Martin had not delivered to Robert Arnot the whole quantity of wood in time, consequently he had to pay the equivalent of the highest market price (ULStA B 10/8/8).

53 This was apparently the case when Thomas Davidson, John Walker, Peter Millar, and John Morton acknowledged their debt of a 'last of flimis byndtreis' to deliver to John Martin by 8 September (ULStA B 10/8/4, 24 March 1567/8).

54 ULStA B 10/8/ 4 23 February and 16 March 1567-8.

55 ULStA B 10/8/8 30 March 1590.

56 Ibid, 7 August 1590.

57 ULStA B 10/8/7 30 August 1581.

58 Lillehammer, A, 'The Scottish-Norwegian Timber Trade in the Stavanger Area in the Sixteenth and Seventeenth Centuries', in Smout, T C ed., *Scotland and Europe, 1200-1850*, (1986, Edinburgh: John Donald), pp 100-3.

59 ULStA B 10/8/4 18 November 1567.

60 ULStA B 10/8/4 30 May 1568.

61 ULStA B 10/8/5 21 June 1569.

62 Ibid, 11 May 1572.

63 Ibid, 15 and 24 April 1571.

64 Ibid, 24 April 1571 (two entries).

65 Ibid.

66 Mentioned as a skipper ibid, 23 September 1571.

67 Ibid, 19 June, 25 July and 31 August 1571.

68 At least part of Melville's cargo appears to have consisted of 4,000 poles ('steyngis'). On 12 April , John Wemyss of Burntisland recognized his obligation to deliver them to Melville in the harbour of Burntisland 'at the side of ane schipe called the *Maria Anna* f.o.b.; Melville was to pay Wemyss £48 by 8 September (ibid, 12 April 1571). It is rather unlikely that the poles should be taken to Norway, rather could one imagine that they should be unloaded in the Northern Isles on the vessel's voyage to Norway.

69 Ibid, 25 April 1571.

70 Ibid, 6 November 1571.

71 Ibid, 20 and 27 November 1571.

72 Ibid, 15 April 1571.

73 ULStA B 10/8/8, 11 April 1590.

74 Ibid, 28 April 1590 (two entries).

75 Ibid, 28 April 1590.

76 This did not exclude the acquisition of wood at Crail; thus James Lauder owed to William Currour inter alia £3 for 150 'girdis', i.e. barrel hoops, ibid, 25 March 1589.

77 Lillehammer, A, 'Boards, Beams and Barrel Hoops: Contacts between Scotland and the Stavanger Area in the Seventeenth Century', in Simpson, G G ed., *Scotland and Scandinavia, 800-1800*, (1990, Edinburgh: John Donald), p 102.

78 'Grit' (=great) salt was foreign salt, small salt Scottish salt. In the early eighteenth century Scottish salt was reckoned as sufficient for the curing of herring for the Baltic market, but not convenient for fish prepared for the markets in the Mediterranean or in the West Indies, see Harris, B, 'Scotland's Herring Fisheries and the Prosperity of the Nation, *c* 1660-1760', *Scottish Historical Review* 79, (2000), pp 47-8; Whatley, CA, *The Scottish Salt Industry 1570-1850, an economic and social history*, (1987, Aberdeen: Aberdeen University Press), pp 34 and 36. Scottish salt was not considered appropriate for the curing of other fish than cod, Whatley, C A, *'That Important and Necessary Article'. The Salt Industry and Its Trade in Fife and Tayside, c. 1570-1850*, Abertay Historical Society Publications no. 22, (1984, Dundee: Dundee Abertay Historical Society), pp 29-30.

79 ULStA B 10/8/4, 8 October 1566.

80 ULStA B 10/8/6. For another example of salt as working capital to be paid in fish, see ibid, 18 September 1576.

81 In April 1583 John Reid obliged himself to deliver to William Annand six barrels train oil ("traine and vlie") by 15 August 1583. Oil was an expensive commodity: On August 29th, 1582 Thomas Beane and Thomas Blair acknowledged their debt of £120 to Thomas Robertson of Dundee as payment for three eights of the crear the *Swallow* with her furniture and half the cargo (timber). As payment they should give Robertson a barrel oil by Christmas 1582 (ULStA B 10/8/7, 29 August 1582 and 23 April 1583).

82 ULStA B 10/8/8, 7 May 1590 (two entries).

83 Ibid, 18 May 1590 (two entries).

84 Ibid., 23 May 1590.

85 Generally, the voyage to Bordeaux in order to fetch the new wine took place late in the year, cf. Boissonade, P, 'Le mouvement commercial entre la France et les Iles britanniques au XVe siècle', *Revue historique* 134, (1920), p 223. See also Martin, C J M, 'Seafaring and Trade in East Fife', in Liszka, T R and Walker, L E M (eds), *The North Sea World in the Middle Ages: Studies in the Cultural History of North-Western Europe*, (2001, Dublin: Four Courts Press), p 172. Thus on 25 August 1580, Alexander Wemyss acknowledged his debt of 50 merks Scots to Alexander Meldrum. In return he obliged himself to furnish to Meldrum two puncheons of Bordeaux claret by 2 February 1580/1 or to pay the highest market price (ULStA B 10/8/6).

86 ULStA B 10/8/8, 16 June 1590.

87 ULStA B 10/8/8, 10 February 1589/90.

88 ULStA B 10/8/5, 9 March 1573/4; *Dictionary of the Older Scottish Tongue* I, p 321, cf. X, p 639.

[89] ULStA B 10/8/6 4 May 1576.

[90] ULStA B 10/8/2, fol. 79 v., 18 December 1559.

[91] Compared with other contracts, it is unusual that the apprentice should be taught by both Galloway and his wife. However, the preparation of bait and lines was female work, and if as a future fisherman Walker should be able to instruct his female helpers, he had to learn this part of the craft as well.

[92] ULStA B 10/8/1, fol. 32 v.-33 r., 19 May 1553; *Dictionary of the Older Scottish Tongue* II, pp 712 and 720, IX, p 162. Hay, E R and Walker, B, *Focus on Fishing: Arbroath & Gourdon*, Abertay Historical Society Publication no. 23, (Dundee 1985: Dundee Abertay Historical Society), p 53. The lifetime of a 'sma'line' was reckoned as one year, ibid., p 81.

[93] ULStA B 10/8/5, 12 October 1569.

[94] Smith, *Shetland Life and Trade,* pp 3-4; Rorke, 'The Scottish Herring Trade', p 161.

[95] ULStA B 10/8/4, 19 October 1567 (£40 borrowed from John Black in Kilrennie to pay by 2 February 1567/8).

[96] Ibid, 29 June 1568.

[97] ULStA B 10/8/6, 4 May 1576. Other cases ULStA B 10/8/8 28 April 1590 (working capital paid in April 1589 for the summer fishing off Shetland), ibid., 30 March 1591 (summer fishing off Shetland), cf ibid, 12 January 1590/1 (loan contracted in May 1590 at Shetland) and 29 December 1590 (salt sent to Shetland in June 1590).

[98] Smith, Shetland Life and Trade, p 15.

[99] ULStA B 10/8/7, 29 April 1583.

[100] Ibid, 2 May 1583.

[101] ULStA B 10/8/6, 16 September 1579 (two entries).

[102] ULStA B 10/8/4, 18 November 1567.

[103] ULStA B 10/8/8, 27 October 1590.

[104] Ibid, 9 February 1590/1.

[105] Ibid, 1 September 1590.

[106] *The Register of the Privy Council of Scotland* I, ed Burton, J H (1877, Edinburgh: H.M. General Register House), p 483 (24 September 1566).

[107] Rorke, 'The Scottish Herring Trade', pp 156 and 161.

[108] Ibid, p. 157.

[109] ULStA B 10/8/4 23 September 1567 and 29 September 1568 (two entries).

[110] Ibid, 23 September 1566 (within two days after their arrival), 8 October 1566.

[111] Ibid, 29 September 1568 (two entries).

[112] Ibid, 4 February 1566/7. As the Loch Broom fishing took place in autumn, it is probable that Buffy had not received the amount before he left.

[113] Ibid, 11 February 1566/7.

[114] Ibid, 13 May 1567.

[115] Ibid, 25 November 1567.

[116] ULStA B 10/8/6 27 May 1578.

[117] ULStA B 65/8/1 29 July 1589.

[118] The issue had been raised by Crail in the Convention of Royal Burghs, where Edinburgh had supported the case, *Records of the Convention of the Royal Burghs of Scotland* I ed Marwick, J D, (1866, Edinburgh: W. Paterson), p 213 (3 May 1586).

[119] *The Register of the Privy Council of Scotland* IV ed Masson, D, (1881, Edinburgh 1881: H.M. General Register House), pp 121-3 (11 November 1586).

[120] Rorke, 'The Scottish Herring Trade', pp 156-7 and 163.

[121] *The Register of the Privy Council of Scotland* II ed Burton, J H (1878, Edinburgh: H.M. General Register House) p 534 (23 June 1576).

[122] *The Register of the Privy Council of Scotland* III ed Masson, D, (1880, Edinburgh: H.M.General Register House pp 124-5 (28 March 1579).

[123] The Register of the Privy Council of Scotland IV, pp 123-4 and 243.

[124] Ibid, p 605 (1 April 1591).

[125] Coull, J R, 'Fisheries in Scotland in the 16th, 17th and 18th Centuries: the evidence in Macfarlane's Geographical Collections' , *Scottish Geographical Magazine* 93, (1977), p 12.

[126] Shaw, F J, The Northern and Western Islands of Scotland: Their Economy and Society in the Seventeenth Century, (1980, Edinburgh: John Donald), pp 125-6.

[127] Coull, J R, 'The Development of Herring Fishing in the Outer Hebrides', *International Journal of Maritime History* 15,2, (2003), p 22.

[128] ULStA B 10/8/5 11 August 1569.

[129] Ibid, 27 September 1569.

[130] Ibid, the same date.

[131] See the tables for Scottish trade to the Baltic 1574-1582 in Riis, *Should Auld Acquaintance Be Forgot* II, pp 29-51.

[132] ULStA B 10/8/5 27 September 1569. Generally, the voyage to Bordeaux was the last international voyage of the year, which allowed the Scots to bring home the new wine, cf. Chapter One, section "Salt" n. 8.

[133] ULStA B 10/8/6 3 April and 22 May 1576.

[134] One should not forget, however, that a volume of the Burgh Court Books comprising the years 1584-1589 has been lost.

[135] ULStA B 10/8/6 17 September 1579 and 23 February 1579/80; B 10/8/7 29 March, 18 April and 30 August 1581; 26 March, 11 April, 27 August 3 and September 1582, cf 6 September 1583.

[136] ULStA B 10/8/6 4 October 1577.

[137] ULStA B 10/8/6 17 September 1579 and 23 February 1579/80.

[138] Ibid.

[139] Ibid, 7 September 1576 and 11 March 1577/8.

[140] ULStA B 10/8/7 30 March 1584.

[141] Ibid, 1 January 1580/1.

[142] ULStA B 10/8/5 1 September 1571.

[143] Ibid, 16 September 1571, obligation by Andro Baxter and Robert Arnot.

[144] Ibid, 4 September 1570.

[145] Ibid, 12 May 1572.

[146] Ibid, 20 September 1572.

[147] Ibid, 18 September 1572. If no fish was to be had, Farmer should pay the amount back within two weeks of his return.

[148] Ibid, 2 September 1573.

[149] Ibid, 20 September 1573. On 9 February 1573/4 Moreis acknowledged a debt of £4 to Andro Baxter for the rent of one eighth of his ship for a voyage to Northern Scotland (ibid).

[150] Ibid, 16 September 1573.

[151] Ibid, 29 September 1576. From the furnisher of capital he had received £ 30, but if no fish was to be had, he should pay back the amount plus an indemnity of £10. In spite of the fact that the herring was from 'Northern Scotland', the fishing ground was mentioned as 'Spraw' or 'Sprall' by Shetland.

[152] Ibid, 7 September 1576 (two entries).

[153] ULStA B 10/8/2, fol. 80 r. 18 December 1559.

[154] ULStA B 10/8/6 18 September 1576.

[155] ULStA B 10/8/6 16 December 1576.

[156] Ibid, 29 April 1578.

[157] ULStA B 10/8/7, 13 February 1582/3.

[158] Ibid, 11 March 1582/3.

[159] Rorke, 'The Scottish Herring Trade', pp 156 and 160-2.

[160] ULStA B 10/8/5 27 August, 4, 7 (two entries), 9, 14, 15 (three entries), 20 (two entries), 27 and 29 September, 14 October 1569; 4, 12, 15, 23, 25, 27 September, and 6 October 1570; 1, 4, 9 and 17 September 1571; 18 September 1572.

[161] Ibid, 11 August 1569.

[162] Ibid, 1 September 1571.

[163] ULStA B 10/8/7, 11 November 1581.

[164] ULStA B 10/8/5, 12 May 1574.

[165] ULStA B 10/8/7 8 March 1580/1. Ling (with the Latin name of *Molva molva*) is a marine fish related to the cod.

[166] Ibid, 2 May 1583.

[167] Ibid, 29 April 1583.

[168] ULStA B 10/8/2 2 October 1555.

[169] ULStA B 10/8/8 13 September 1590.

[170] ULStA B 10/8/4, 30 April 1567.

[171] ULStA B 10/8/7, 2 May 1583.

[172] ULStA B 10/8/4, 4 March 1566/7 and 23 February 1567/8.

[173] Kind information from Keracher, fishmonger, St Andrews.

[174] *The Scottish National Dictionary* VII, ed Grant, W, and Murison, D D, (1968, Edinburgh), pp 19-20, article 'palie', senses I 2 and II 2.

[175] ULStA B 10/8/7, 8 September 1583.

[176] ULStA B 10/8/1 19 May 1553 and ULStA B 10/8/6, 4 May 1576 and 25 February 1577/8.

[177] ULStA B 10/8/1 19 May 1553; ULStA B 10/8/6 4 May 1576.

[178] ULStA B 10/8/8 10 February 1589/90.

[179] ULStA B 10/8/5 9 March 1573/4 and B 10/8/6 4 May 1576.

[180] Smith, Shetland Life and Trade, p. 25.

[181] Rorke, 'The Scottish Herring Trade', pp 150-1.

[182] ULStA B 10/8/7, 9 August 1583.

[183] ULStA B 10/8/6 26 May 1579.

[184] Ibid, 20 August 1580.

[185] ULStA B 10/8/7 31 August 1582. Only a few years earlier the Privy Council had authorised Crail to levy extra duties for a period of three years in order to finance the, 'building of the bulwark, port, and havin.' Of each 'tun gudis' two shillings were to be paid at the entrance to or departure from Crail, likewise was one shilling due at the entrance or departure of each 'tun of fraucht.' Of timber a duty of 1 % was to be paid, *Register of the Privy Council of Scotland* II, p 431, 3 February 1574/5.

[186] Ibid, 8 January 1582/3.

[187] Ibid, 21 May 1583.

[188] ULStA B 10/8/5, 31 October 1570.

[189] Ibid, 1 June 1571.

[190] Ibid, 21 November 1570.

[191] Smith, Shetland Life and Trade, pp 3-4.

[192] ULStA B 10/8/8 12 January 1590/1.

[193] Ibid, 2 March 1590/1.

[194] ULStA B 10/8/ 6 22 May 1576.

[195] Smith, *Shetland Life and Trade,* pp 3-4, 15, and 19.

[196] ULStA B 10/8/7, 17 February 1581/2.

[197] Ibid, 25 June 1583. The modest sum compared with 1581 for the same quantity indicates that the 14s. could have been the last instalment of a larger sum.

[198] Brown, C, *Scottish Regional Recipes*, (1981, Glasgow: The Molendinar Press), p 73.

[199] ULStA B 10/8/8, 18 November 1589.

[200] ULStA B 10/8/7 8 March 1580/1.

[201] NAS E 71/6/1-10: Customs Books of Pittenweem, Anstruther, and Crail.; the customs books E 71/6/6 and E 71/6/7 are identical.

[202] NAS E 71/6/11, fol. 1 r.-v.

[203] NAS E 71/6/8, (William Symson's account), fol. 2 r.-4 v..

[204] NAS. E 71/6/9 Cocket Book 14 November 1576-18 November 1577, fol. 2 r.-5 r.

[205] For most of the period covered by the customs account beginning on 17 December 1574, the corresponding Burgh Court Book is missing.

[206] See Table 8.

[207] NAS E 71/6/9, fol. 2 v.

[208] Loc. cit.

[209] ULStA B 10/8/6, 18 and 21 September 1577.

[210] See Tables 8 and 9.

[211] In 1577 Robert Arnot obliged himself to deliver 18 barrels herring by (one last alone and one with Steven Arnot), and William Arnot obliged himself to furnish two lasts of herring; as the term of delivery was Christmas 1577 (see Table 9), they could hardly have been entered in the Cocket Book November 1576-November 1577.

[212] NAS. E 71/6/5: Customs Book 26 December 1573 to 6 March 1575 (=1574/5), fol. 4 r.-v..

[213] NAS. E 71/6/1: Customs Book 1557, fol. 1 r.-v.

[214] Ibid., fol. 2 r.-3 v.

[215] Smith, Shetland Life and Trade, pp. 3-4.

[216] In order to enable future researchers to check and possibly correct the figures, the names of the persons who declared their herring at Dundee and Edinburgh are given.

[217] The increasing value of herring since the 1580s must have been caused by the deterioration of the currency since *c* 1570, cf. Devine, T M and Lythe, S G E, 'The economy of Scotland under James VI', *Scottish Historical Review* 50, (1971), p 94 and Gibson, A J S and Smout, T C, *Prices, Food and Wages in Scotland 1550-1780*, (1995, Cambridge: Cambridge University Press), p 15.

[218] Bochove, C van, 'The ‚Golden Mountain': An Economic Analysis of Holland's Early Modern Herring Fisheries', in: Sicking, L and Abreu-Ferreira, D (eds), *Beyond the Catch: Fisheries in the North Atlantic, the North Sea, and the Baltic, 900-1850*, (2009, Leiden-Boston: Brill), pp 212 and 220-1.

[219] ULStA B 10/8/6, 27 August 1578.

[220] ULStA B 10/8/2, fol. 79 v., 18 December 1559.

[221] Rorke, M 'The Scottish Herring Trade, 1470-1600', *Scottish Historical Review* 84, (2005), p 152.

[222] Ibid, p 155.

[223] Ibid, p 161.

[224] ULStA B 10/8/4, 4 February 1566/7.

[225] Ibid, 13 May 1567.

[226] ULStA B 10/8/5, 12 October 1569.

[227] Ibid, 9 February 1573/4.

[228] ULStA B 10/8/6, 8 September 1576.

229 Rorke, 'The Scottish Herring Trade' , p 161. In 1586 a ship of Pittenweem had been furnished for a voyage to Loch Broom for £228-13-4 (ibid, p 162).

230 ULStA B 10/8/5, 1 April 1572.

231 ULStA B 10/8/6, 7 September 1576.

232 Ibid, same day, partners John Martyne, James Cass and James Dingwall.

233 Ibid, 30 August 1577.

234 Dundee Shipping Lists, pp 220-1 (4 February 1588/9) and 225 (undated 1589 ?).

235 Ibid, p 209 (24 July 1583).

236 Ibid, pp 204 (11 August 1581), 218 (3 September 1588), 226 (no date 1589, three entries) and 228 (7 November 1589).

237 Fenton, A, *The Northern Isles: Orkney and Shetland*, (1978, Edinburgh: Donald), p 574.

238 Ballantyne, J H, and Smith, B (eds), *Shetland Documents 1195-1579*, (1999, Lerwick: Shetland Islands Council & Shetland Times), p 296.

239 Gibson and Smout, *Prices, Food and Wages in Scotland 1550-1780*, pp 41, 371 and 373. Speaking of the fiars' prices Gibson and Smout found it reasonable to estimate a boll of oatmeal in Fife *c* 1570 at £3 (ibid, p 84), which would correspond to 3s. 9d. (45d.) the peck.

240 Ibid, p 69.

241 Ibid, p 77.

242 Ibid, pp 225-60 and 339. In the diets mentioned brandy appears only in that of Scottish soldiers *c* 1689, ibid, p 253.

243 ULStA B 10/8/5; cf ibid, 29 January (two entries) and 5 February 1571/2. Also before 1 June 1571 an unfree man had to pay 6s. per last, ibid, 23 January 1570/1.

244 ULStA B 10/8/7, 8 January 1582/3.

245 ULStA B 10/8/6.

246 ULStA B 10/8/7, 31 August 1582.

247 ULStA B 10/8/5, 21 November 1570.

248 Riis, Should Auld Acquaintance Be Forgot I, p 33.

249 Ibid, I, p 40.

250 ULStA B 10/8/8, 9 February 1590/1.

251 Ibid, 12 January 1590/1.

[252] Secher, V A (ed), *Corpus Constitutionum Daniæ. Forordninger, Recesser og andre kongelige Breve, Danmarks Lovgivning vedkommende* I, (1887, Copenhagen: Selskabet for Udgivelse af Kilder til dansk Historie), p 535 no 640.

[253] ULStA B 10/8/5, 16 September 1570; B 10/8/7 17 November 1581; 7 (two entries) and 13 September 1582; 27 August , 3, 6 (two entries), 8 (three entries), 10, 14, 17 (two entries), 18 and 19 September 1583; B 10/8/81 September 1590.

[254] ULStA B 10/8/5 7 September 1569.

[255] Ibid, 23 and 27 September 1570.

[256] Ibid., 25 September 1570.

[257] ULStA B 10/8/8, 12 September 1589.

[258] ULStA B 10/8/7, 13 February 1582/3.

[259] ULStA B 10/8/5, 3 and 7 July 1569.

[260] ULStA B 10/8/4.

[261] Ibid.

[262] ULStA B 10/8/8 (16 June 1590).

[263] Probably in 1570 Thomas Hall cleared three lasts of herring and 800 fish and must thus have had other contractors than the partnership, see NAS. E 71/6/3: Cocket Book Crail, Anstruther, Pittenweem 30 September 1570-10 October 1572, fol. 2 verso and 5 verso. In 1574-5 he entered thirteen lasts of packed keiling, NAS. E 71/6/8: Customs Account Pittenweem, Crail and Anstruther 3 November 1574-9 November 1575 (customs officer William Symson), fol. 6 recto.

[264] ULStA B 10/8/5 (12 and 23 September 1570).

[265] ULStA B 10/8/6 (7 and 21 September 1576).

[266] NAS. E 71/6/2: Customs Book Pittenweem, Anstruther, Crail 1566, fol. 9 recto. The herring was also entered in the cocket book of Dundee (NAS. E 71/12/7 fol. 6 verso, 1 February 1566/7).

[267] Ramsay was a merchant of Dundee, who was admitted a burgess in 1559, cf Dundee City Archives, Lockit Book of Burgesses of Dundee 1513-1981, 4 October 1559.

[268] NAS. E 71/12/7 Dundee Entry Book of Cockets 1566-7, fol. 5 recto (9 [December] 1566), fol. 6 recto (22 February 1566/7) and 6 verso (1 February 1566/7).

[269] ULStA B 10/8/7 (8 September 1583).

[270] Cf. Smout, T C and Stewart, M *The Firth of Forth. An Environmental History* (2012, Edinburgh, Birlinn Limited) , pp 29-30.

271 ULStA B 10/8/6, 6, 9 and 16 September 1577.

272 Ibid, 22 May 1576.

273 ULStA B 10/8/5 (15 September 1570).

274 Ibid, 16 September 1571.

275 Ibid, 16 September 1574.

276 ULStA B 10/8/6 (8 and 9 May 1576).

277 Ibid, 7 and 12 September 1576.

278 Ibid, 18 April and 10 May 1577.

279 Gray does not appear in the Sound Toll Registers 1574-83, which obviously does not exclude other destinations.

280 ULStA B 10/8/6 (20 April 1577).

281 Ibid, 9 September 1577.

282 Ibid. 16 September 1577.

283 Ibid, 6 September 1577.

284 Ibid, 16 September 1577.

285 Ibid, 30 November 1577.

286 Ibid, 19 November 1579.

287 Ibid, 6 May 1580.

288 ULStA B 10/8/7 (21 March 1580/1 and 18 April 1581).

289 Ibid, 30 August 1581 (two entries).

290 Ibid, 2 September 1581.

291 Ibid, 22 November 1581.

292 Ibid, 15 November 1581.

293 Ibid, 19 November 1581.

294 Ibid, 17 November 1581.

295 Ibid, 26 March 1582.

296 Ibid, 18 and 21 September 1582.

297 Ibid, 3 and 13 September 1582.

298 Ibid, 7 September 1582.

299 Ibid, 24 September 1582.

300 Ibid, 13 February 1582/3.

301 Ibid, 11 March 1582/3.

[302] Ibid, 3 December 1583 (date of registration, the date of the obligation was 2 September 1583).

[303] Ibid, 25 January 1583/4.

[304] Ibid, 16 March 1583/4.

[305] ULStA B 10/8/5 (11 August and 7 September 1569; 1 September 1571); B 10/8/6 (7 and 15 September 1576); B 10-8-7 (29 April 1583).

[306] ULStA B 10/8/5 (2 September 1573). Since 1569, when Baxter had been at Loch Carron on board John Davidson's ship, he must have acquired his own crear.

[307] Riis, Should Auld Acquaintance Be Forgot I, p 40.

[308] RA. Øresundstoldregnskab 1562, p 368 (11 June).

[309] RA. Øresundstoldregnskab 1576 (Frederik Lyall), pp 298 and 310 (24 May and 3 July).

[310] RA. Øresundstoldregnskab 1578, pp 343 and 359.

[311] RA. Øresundstoldregnskab 1577, pp 35, 352 and 357 (6 June two entries, and 5 July).

[312] RA. Øresundstoldregnskab 1580, pp 304 and 321 (14 May and 6 July).

[313] Ibid, pp 40, 297 and 308 (21 April, two entries, and 8 June).

[314] RA. Øresundstoldregnskab 1583, p 390 (10 June ).

[315] RA. Øresundstoldregnskab 1 May 1587 to 1 May 1588, pp 423 and 445, cf pp 1307 and 1312 (8 July and 7 August 1587).

[316] RA. Øresundstoldregnskab 1 May 1589 – 1 May 1590 (Morten Jensen), p 405 (28 May 1589).

[317] ULStA B 10/8/7 (27 August 1582).

[318] NAS. E 71/6/3: Cocket Book Crail, Anstruther, Pittenweem 30 September 1570 – 10 October 1572, fol. 3 recto.

[319] RA. Øresundstoldregnskab 1 May 1587-1 May 1588, pp 388/1298 and 406/1302 (1 May and 3 June 1587). The value of the Scottish goods, 834 daler, clearly exceeded that of the rye (544 daler).

[320] RA. Øresundstoldregnskab 1 May 1588-1 May 1589, fol. 167 recto and 170 verso (4 May and 11 June 1588).

[321] ULStA B 10/8/6 (24 November 1579) and B 10-8-7 (9 May 1581).

[322] Ibid, B 10/8/5 (21 June 1569).

[323] See the following section.

[324] ULStA B 10/8/6 (3 April 1576).

[325] RA. Øresundstoldregnskab 1576, pp 288 and 299. The values of his cargoes were 850 (from Flushing), respectively 742 daler (from Danzig).

[326] RA. Øresundstoldregnskab 1578, pp 339 and 354.

[327] Ibid, pp 345 and 360 (25 April and 27 May).

[328] RA. Øresundstoldregnskab 1585, pp 46 and 316 (13 May) and 337 (14 August).

[329] ULSt A B 10/8/6 (24 November 1579). Even if in the usual sense Davidson was no contractor, I have included him in Table 20, as he worked for the merchant George Meldrum.

[330] ULStA B 10/8/5 (27 September 1569).

[331] ULStA B 10/8/4 (7 January two entries, 14 and 31 January 1566/7).

[332] ULStA B 10/8/5 (20 March 1570/1).

[333] ULStA B 10/8/6 (5 May 1576, calendared in Ballantyne, J H and Smith, B eds., *Shetland Documents 1195-1579*, (1999 Lerwick: Shetland Islands Council & Shetland Times), pp 172-3 no. 225).

[334] ULStA B 10/8/6 (3 September 1576), and Table 20.

[335] ULStA B 10/8/7 (1 January 1580/1).

[336] RA. Øresundstoldregnskab 1567, p 369 (9 April and 14 May ). Coming from Scotland, he cleared six lasts of herring and returned with pitch and tar, ashes, iron, flax and hemp.

[337] RA. Øresundstoldregnskab 1578, pp 358 and 375 (23 May and 23 June).

[338] RA. Øresundstoldregnskab 1580, pp 304 and 313.

[339] Riis, Should Auld Acquaintance Be Forgot, II, pp 29-51.

[340] RA. Øresundstoldregnskab 1581, pp 325 and 339.

[341] RA. Øresundstoldregnskab 1 May 1587-1 May 1588, pp 386/1297 and 403/1301 (1 May and 2 June 1587).

[342] Register of the Privy Council of Scotland 1st Series III, ed. David Masson, (1880 Edinburgh: H. M. General Register House) p 616 (August 1583).

[343] ULStA B 10/8/6 (30 August 1577).

[344] ULStA B 10/8/5 (17 June 1572).

[345] Riis, T 'Navigation et formation des marins en Ecosse vers 1600', in *Horizons marins – Itinéraires spirituels (Mélanges Michel Mollat)* II, (1987, Paris: Publications de la Sorbonne) pp 301-2.

[346] ULStA B 10/8/4 (22 January 1567/8).

[347] NAS. E 71/6/6. Customs Book Crail, Anstruther, Pittenweem 31 March to 3 November 1574, customs officer William Symson, fol. 7 recto.

[348] NAS. E 71/6/8: Customs Book Pittenweem, Crail and Anstruther 3 November 1574 – 9 November 1575, customs officer William Symson, fol. 9 verso.

[349] ULStA B 10/8/6 (8 September 1576).

[350] NAS. E 71/6/9: Cocket Book Crail, Anstruther, Pittenweem 14 November 1576 – 18 November 1577, fol. 11 recto.

[351] ULStA B 10/8/4 (30 May 1568). In the same year he sent timber with a Dutch skipper, but neither the destination nor the port of departure is known (ibid, 7 December 1568).

[352] ULStA B 10/8/5 (21 June 1569).

[353] Ibid, 24 April (four entries), 19 June, 25 July, and 31 August 1571, cf 12 April 1571.

[354] Ibid, 15 April 1571.

[355] Ibid, 6 November 1571.

[356] Ibid, 11 May 1572.

[357] Ibid, 20 November 1571.

[358] ULStA B 10/8/6 (4 April 1578).

[359] Ibid, 27 August 1578.

[360] Ibid, 3 November 1576.

[361] ULStA B 10/8/7 (30 August 1581, two entries).

[362] ULStA B 10/8/8 (25 March 1589).

[363] Ibid, 11 April 1590.

[364] Ibid, 28 April 1590 (two entries).

[365] Ibid, 28 April 1590.

[366] Ibid , 24 November 1590.

[367] Ibid, 6 July 1591. The sense of 'skenis treeis' is not clear. Perhaps wooden hafts for daggers (skeans) were meant.

[368] ULStA B 10/8/4 (25 November 1567).

[369] ULStA B 10/8/6 (12 April 1580).

[370] ULStA B 10/8/7 (3 September 1581).

[371] ULStA B 10/8/6 (26 August and 8 September 1577).

[372] Ibid, 12 May 1580.

[373] Ibid, 19 September 1578, cf ibid, 4 May 1579.

[374] Ibid, 1 and 3 September 1577.

[375] Ibid, 9, 17 and 24 September 1577.

376  Ibid, 30 August, 14 (two entries) and 15 September 1580.

377  ULStA B 10/8/7 (21 March 1580/1).

378  Ibid, 13 and 14 September 1581.

379  Ibid, 30 December 1581, 27 February 1581/2, and 26 March 1582 (two entries).

380  Ibid, 1 June 1582, referring to a contract of 18 April 1582.

381  Ibid, 3 September 1582.

382  NAS. E 71/12/9 Dundee Customs Account 3 December 1577- 21 January 1578/9, fol. 2 verso, 3 verso, 10 recto, 11 recto and 15 recto and E 71/12/10 Dundee Cocket Book 21 January 1578/9 – 15 January 1579/80, fol. 4 recto, 8 recto and 14 recto.

383  ULStA B 10/8/7 (6 September 1583, two entries).

384  Dundee City Archives, Register of Ships 1580-1589 = Miller, A H (ed) *The Compt Buik of David Wedderburne Merchant of Dundee 1587-1630. Together with the Shipping Lists of Dundee 1580-1618*, (Scottish History Society XXVIII), (1898: Edinburgh), pp 214 and 217 (28 March 1584 and 27 August 1588).

385  NAS. E 71/12/10 Dundee Cocket Book 21 January 1578/9-15 January 1579/80, fol. 8 verso, 9 recto, 10 recto, 11 recto and 12 recto.

386  NAS. E 71/12/11 Dundee Customs Account 12 August to 1 October 1582, fol. 3 recto-verso.

387  NAS. E 71/6/2: Customs Book Pittenweem, Anstruther, Crail 1566, fol. 9 verso.

388  ULStA B 10/8/4 (29 September, two entries).

389  ULStA B 10/8/5 (15, 26, and 29 September 1569).

390  RA. Øresundstoldregnskab 1569, pp 277 and 295 (6 June and 14 July).

391  ULStA B 10-8-5 (23 September 1570).

392  Ibid, 4 September 1571.

393  Ibid, 12 May 1572.

394  ULStA B 10/8/6 (17 May and 7 September 1576; 9 September 1577).

395  ULStA B 10/8/7 (8 September 1581; 7 October 1582).

396  They were mentioned as a married couple in 1566 (ULStA B 10/8/4, 24 September 1566).

397  ULStA B 10/8/8 (7, 15, and 28 September 1590).

398  Ibid, 1, 18, and 22 (seven entries) September 1590.

399  ULStA B 10/8/5 (9, 10 (two entries) and 21 September 1574).

[400] ULStA B 10/8/6 (12, 14, 16, and 19 September 1576).

[401] As note 17.

[402] ULStA B 10/8/8 1 (Andro Davidson) and 22 (Edward Abbey) September.

[403] ULStA B 10/8/6 (25 March 1580).

[404] ULStA B 10/8/7 (8 March 1580/1).

[405] ULStA B 10/8/5 (4 September 1569).

[406] Ibid, 7 July 1569.

[407] Burton J H (ed), *Register of the Privy Council of Scotland* 1st Series III (1880, Edinburgh, H.M.General Register House), pp 102-3 (28 February 1578/9).

[408] ULStA B 10/8/5 (27 and 28 September 1569).

[409] In medieval trading partnerships the *socius stans* is the (often elder) partner who stays at home whereas the *socius itinerans* travels with the goods.

[410] ULStA B 10/8/5, 5 January 1571/2.

[411] Ibid, 23 September 1571.

[412] Ibid, 13 September 1571 (two entries).

[413] Ibid, 18 September 1572.

[414] Ibid, 20 September 1572 (two entries).

[415] Ibid, 4 and 6 September 1573.

[416] Ibid, 16 September 1573.

[417] ULStA B 10/8/6 (7 April 1576).

[418] This is confirmed by his other activities: in 1578/9-1579/80 he entered fifty skins and fifty schoirlings at Dundee (NAS. E 71/12/10 Dundee Cocket Book 21 January 1578/9 – 15 January 1579/80, fol. 4 recto and 8 recto), in 1589-90 he paid £3-8 for English goods entered at Edinburgh (NAS. E 71/30/22 Edinburgh Customs Account 1 October 1589 – 1 October 1590, fol. 49 verso).

[419] ULStA B 10/8/6 10 October 1576.

[420] Ibid, 20 January 1576/7, cf. 15 December 1576 (Currour's obligation to William Annand).

[421] NAS. E 71/32/9 Edinburgh Entry Book of Cockets 10 September 1580 – 1 August 1581, fol. 4 recto (four lasts of herring entered at Edinburgh) and E 71/12/9 Dundee Customs Account 3 December 1577-21 January 1578/9, fol. 16 recto (six barrels herring entered at Dundee).

[422] ULStA B 10/8/6 27 March 1576.

[423] Ibid, 15 December 1576, 1 February 1576/7 and 27 May 1577.

[424] Ibid, 27 August 1578.

[425] Ibid, 22 April 1578.

[426] ULStA B 10/8/7 20 April 1583.

[427] Ibid, 9 August 1583.

[428] ULStA B 10/8/6 17 September 1579.

[429] ULStA B 10/8/7 30 April 1582.

[430] ULStA B 10/8/5 (13 and 15 September 1570).

[431] See preceding section. Melville also advanced £50 to Morton in view of his planned two voyages to Norway (ibid, 24 April 1571).

[432] ULStA B 10/8/5 (9 and 15 April 1571).

[433] Ibid, 4 December 1571.

[434] Ibid, 2 September 1573 and 16 February 1573/4.

[435] NAS. E 71/6/5: Customs Book Crail, Anstruther, Pittenweem 26 December 1573-6 March 1575, fol. 2 recto.

[436] NAS. E 71/6/8: Customs Book Pittenweem, Crail and Anstruther 3 November 1574-9 November 1575, fol. 4 recto and 6 recto.

[437] NAS. E 71/6/9: Cocket Book Crail, Anstruther, Pittenweem 14 November 1576-18 November 1577, fol. 11 verso.

[438] ULStA B 10/8/6 (27 May 1578).

[439] ULStA B 10/8/5 (19 and 20 October 1569).

[440] Ibid, 7 September 1569 (three entries).

[441] NAS. E 71/12/10 Dundee Cocket Book 21 January 1578/9-15 January 1579/80, fol. 2 recto, 3 recto-verso and 7 verso.

[442] Dundee City Archives, Lockit Book of Burgesses of Dundee 1513-1981 (no pagination).

[443] ULStA B 10/8/5 (12 May 1574) and B 10-8-8 (13 September 1590).

[444] NAS. E 71/6/5 Customs Book Crail, Anstruther Pittenweem 26 December 1573-6 March 1575, fol. 11 recto; E 71/6/8 Customs Book Pittenweem, Crail and Anstruther 3 November 1574-9 November 1575, fol. 4 recto and 5 recto; ULStA B 10/8/6 (17 September 1579).

[445] ULStA B 65/8/1, Burgh Court Book St Andrews February 1588/9 - 14 November 1592, no pagination, date 23 September 1589.

[446] ULStA B 10/8/6 (30 August 1580) and B 10/8/7 (17 September 1583).

[447] ULStA B 10/8/5 (23 September 1570) and B 10/8/7 (12 June 1581); NAS. E 71/6/10 Customs Account Crail 21 August-1 October 1582, fol. 3 verso.

448 ULStA B 10/8/6 (7 September 1576, three entries; 4 October 1577, and 6 May 1580, two entries).

449 NAS. E 71/32/10 Edinburgh Entry Book of Cockets 1 October 1589-[1 October 1590], fol. 4 recto.

450 ULStA B 10/8/5 (3 September 1569; 21 August and 12 September 1570; 8 and 10 (two entries) September 1571); NAS. E 71/6/3 Cocket Book Crail, Anstruther, Pittenweem 30 September 1570-10 October 1572, fol. 2 verso and 6 recto.

451 Burton J H (ed), *Register of the Privy Council of Scotland*, 1st Series I, (1877 Edinburgh: H.M. General Register House), pp 528-9 (9 July 1567).

452 Lynch, M *Edinburgh and the Reformation*, (1981, Edinburgh: John Donald), pp. 314 and 374.

453 Ibid, pp. 275, 299, 368, and 378. For the Ruthven raid, see Lynch, M, *Scotland. A New History*, 2nd ed., (1992, London: Pimlico), pp 232-3.

454 Lynch, *Edinburgh and the Reformation*, pp 275, 370 and 379; Marwick, J D (ed) *Extracts from the Records of the Burgh of Edinburgh* V A.D. 1573-1589, 1882, Edinburgh: xxxx, p. 579.

455 NAS. E 71/30/21 Edinburgh Customs Account 1 October 1579-1 October1580, fol.18 verso, 19 recto, 20 verso, 21 verso, 23 verso, 47 recto–48 recto, 49s recto, 51 verso, 59 recto.

456 NAS. E 71/32/10 Edinburgh Entry Book of Cockets 1/10 1589-[1 October 1590], no pagination.

457 NAS. E 71/30/22 Edinburgh Customs Accounts 1 October 1589-1 October 1590, fol. 34 verso, 37 verso, 39 verso, 42 verso, 44 recto, 45 recto, 46 verso.

458 ULStA B 10/8/7 (30 November 1583).

459 Lynch, *Edinburgh and the Reformation*, pp 248, 251, 254-5, 268, 273, 306, and 378.

460 Extracts from the Records of the Burgh of Edinburgh V, pp 437-9 and 579.

461 Ibid, pp 418-20 and 422-3 (20 and 26 May , 4 June 1585). On the moor, see Bryce, W M 'The Burgh Muir of Edinburgh from the Records' , *The Book of the Old Edinburgh Club* 10, (1918), pp 1-263.

462 NAS. E71/30/19 Edinburgh Customs Account 1 October 1575-1 October 1576, fol. 32 verso, 37 verso, 67 recto and 71 recto.

463 NAS. E71/30/20 Edinburgh Customs Account 1 October 1578-1 October 1579, no pagination.

464 NAS.E71/30/22 Edinburgh Customs Account 1 October 1589-1 October 1590, fol. 43 recto.

465 Lynch, *Edinburgh and the Reformation*, pp 236-7, 241, 244, 246, 248-9, 265, 269, 310, 365, and 378; *Extracts from the Records of the Burgh of Edinburgh* V, pp 352-4, 437-9 and 579.

466 Lynch, Edinburgh and the Reformation, p 310.

467 NAS. E71/30/18 Edinburgh Customs Account 15 December 1573-1 November 1574, fol. 5 verso and 17 verso.

468 NAS. E71/30/19 Edinburgh Customs Account 1 October 1575-1 October 1576, fol. 22 recto and 71 recto.

469 *Extracts from the Records of the Burgh of Edinburgh* V, pp 93-4 and 129 (15 December 1578 and 4 December 1579).

470 Ibid, p 32 (11 and 22 December 1574).

471 Ibid, p 362 (4 November 1584).

472 Lynch, Edinburgh and the Reformation, p 381.

473 Extracts from the Records of the Burgh of Edinburgh V, pp 160-1 (29 April 1580).

474 NAS. E71/30/19 Edinburgh Customs Account 1 October 1575-1 October 1576, fol. 18 verso and 59 recto.

475 NAS. E71/30/20 1 October 1578-1 October 1579, pp 2 (herring/codling), 12 (hides) and no pagination (salmon).

476 NAS. E71/32/10 Edinburgh Entry Book of Cockets 1 October 1589-[1 October 1590], no pagination.

477 NAS. E71/30/21 Edinburgh Customs Account 1 October 1579-1 October 1580, fol. 51 verso; NAS. E71/30/22 Edinburgh Customs Account 1 October 1589-1 October 1590, no pagination.

478 Lynch, Edinburgh and the Reformation, p 360.

479 NAS. E71/30/21 Edinburgh Customs Account 1 October 1579-1 October 1580, fol. 51 recto-verso (the account does not distinguish between herring and codling).

480 Edinburgh City Archives SL 150/1/2 Burgh Court Book Canongate 1574-1577, p 234 (10 September 1575).

481 Ibid. SL 150/1/3: Burgh Court Book Canongate 1577-1580, p 433 (11 December 1579); ibid, SL 150/1/4: Burgh Court Book Canongate 1580-1583, pp 6 and 323 (28 November 1580 and 31 October 1582).

482 NAS. E71/30/21 Edinburgh Customs Account 1 October 1579-1 October 1580, fol. 61 recto.

[483] Edinburgh City Archives SL 150/1/2: Burgh Court Book Canongate 1574-1577, p 234 (10 September 1575).

[484] Ibid, SL 150/1/3: Burgh Court Book Canongate 1577-1580, p 1.

[485] Ibid, p 164 (13 June 1578).

[486] Ibid, SL 150/1/4: Burgh Court Book of the Canongate 1580-1583, p 396 (2 March 1582/3).

[487] LeRoy Ladurie, E, *Montaillou, village occitan de 1294 à 1324*, (1975, Paris: Gallimard).

[488] M'Neill, G P (ed), *Rotuli Scaccarium Regum Scotorum, The Exchequer Rolls of Scotland* XXI, (1901, Edinburgh), pp lix-lx and 561-4.

[489] Riis, T 'The Baltic Trade of Montrose in the Sixteenth & Seventeenth Centuries from the Danish Sound Toll Registers', in Jackson, G and Lythe, S G E (eds) *The Port of Montrose. A history of its harbour, trade and shipping* (1993, Tayport, Hutton Press), pp 110-4.

# Tables

Table 1.    Prices for one last herring in pounds Flemish, France 1577

| | |
|---|---|
| Dutch herring | 24.10 pounds |
| Yarmouth herring | 20.12 pounds |
| Irish herring | 18.0 pounds |
| Scottish and coastal herring | 11.0 pounds |

*Source: Poulsen, B, Dutch Herring. An Environmental History, c. 1600-1860 (2008, Amsterdam: Uitgeverij Aksant), p 131, note 1.*

Table 2.    The price of Flemish barrels in £Scots per last 1568, 1570-2, 1577-8, 1581-3, 1590-1 (calendar years)

| | Minimum | Maximum | Average | Entries |
|---|---|---|---|---|
| 1568 | 3-0-0 | 5-0-0 | 4-3-9 | 4 |
| 1570 | 3-10-0 | 4-2-0 | 3-11-0 | 2 |
| 1571 | - | - | 4-0-0 | 3 |
| 1572 | - | - | 4-10-0 | 1 |
| 1577 | 3-6-8 | 5-0-0 | 4-8-11 | 3 |
| 1578 | 3-0-0 | 6-0-0 | 4-10-0 | 2 |
| 1581 | - | - | 4-0-0 | 1 |
| 1582 | - | - | 6-13-4 | 1 |
| 1583 | - | - | 6-0-0 | 1 |
| 1590 | - | - | 4-0-0 | 3 |
| 1591 | - | - | 5-0-0 | 1 |

B 10/8/5 24 and 31 October 1570; 9 April, 11 September and 4 December 1571; 19 February 1571/2; B 10/8/6 20 January 1576/7, 22 and 27 May 1577; 4 April and 27 August 1578; B 10/8/7 25 April 1581; 11 April 1582; 22 January 1582/3; B 10/8/8 24 November 1590; 6 July 1591.

*Source: ULStA B 10/8/4 23 March 1567/8, 30 March, 1 and 22 June and 13 July 1568*

Table 3.   Fish cleared at Crail, Anstruther, and Pittenweem 1557, 1566, 1570-82
(various years)

| | Herring, barrels | Keiling, barrels | Salt keiling, pieces | Salmon, barrels | Fish unspecified, barrels | Fish unspecified, pieces | Pale fish, pieces |
|---|---|---|---|---|---|---|---|
| 1557 | 739 | 1,111 (a) | - | 24 | - | - | - |
| 1566 | 2,427 (b) | 62 | 29,200 | - | - | - | - |
| 30 Sept 1570 – 10 Oct. 1572 (c) | 3,959 | - | - | - | 100 | 81,000 | - |
| 26 Dec 1573 – 6 Mar 1575 (d) | 2,335 (e) | 228 (f) | - | 16 | - | - | 10,000 |
| 31 March – 3 Nov 1574 (g) | 651 | 138 | - | - | 12 (h) | - | 69,500 i |
| 22 Oct – 27 Dec 1574 (j) | - | - | - | - | 156 | 6,200 | - |
| 3 Nov 1574 – 9 Nov 1575 (k) | 4,121 (l) | 488 | - | - | - | - | 42,400 |
| 14 Nov 1576 – 18 Nov 1577 (m) | 5,405 (n) | - | - | - | - | - | 42,300 |
| 21 Aug – 1 Oct 1582 (o) | 2,604 (p) | - | - | - | - | - | 4,000 |

a) Fol. 2 r. sum 13 lasts, *recte* 13 lasts 1 barrel; fol. 2 v. sum 49 lasts, *recte* 48 lasts 2 barrels; fol. 3 r. sum 14 lasts 3 barrels, some figures missing; fol. 3 v. sum 16 lasts. Keiling total according to account 92 lasts 7 barrels. b) Fol. 2 r. sum 23 lasts 4 barrels, *recte* 25 lasts 4 barrels; fol. 2 v. sum 29 lasts 3 barrels, *recte* 20 lasts 3 barrels. c) E 71/6/3, account audited on 10 October 1572 (fol. 10 r.). d) E 71/6/5. e) Sum given fol. 5 r. as 207 lasts 10 barrels, *recte* 194 lasts 7 barrels. f) Fol. 6 r. sum 20 lasts *recte* 19 lasts. Sums given in E 71/6/5 fol. 6 r. and in E 71/6/6 fol. 3 v. and added as 31 lasts 6 barrels (= 378 barrels), *recte* 30 lasts 6 barrels. g) E 71/6/6, identical with E 71/6/7 (accounts by William Symson). h) 1 last 'soundis'. i) According to E 71/6/7 fol. 2 v. the entries refer to the period 31 March to 11 November 1574 . j) E 71/6/4, according to fol. 2 r. account by Thomas Ramsay, customs officer at Crail, from 1 September 1574 to his discharge (no date). k) E 71/6/8 (account by William Symson). l) 775 barrels from Loch Carron and Lewis (fol. 2 r. sum 68 lasts 7 barrels, *recte* 64 lasts 7 barrels), 564 barrels from Loch Carron, 2,782 barrels from the Firth of Forth. m) E 71/6/9 Cocket Book. n) 3,459 barrels from Loch Broom (total given fol. 3 v. as 253 lasts 6 barrels, *recte* 288 lasts 3 barrels), 1,884 barrels from the Firth of Forth. o) E 71/6/10. p) Fol. 2 r. sum 57 lasts 8 barrels *recte* 57 lasts 4 barrels; fol. 2 v. sum 46 lasts 6 barrels *recte* 51 lasts 6 barrels. The total given fol. 3 v. 192 lasts 4 barrels, *recte* 217 lasts.

*Source: NAS E 71/6/1-10.*

Table 4.   Obligations and quantities declared at Crail November 1576-
November 1577 (barrels)

|  | **Customs Book** | **Obligations** |
|---|---|---|
| William Annand | 72 | 36 |
| Robert Arnot | 60 | 42 |
| William Arnot | 144 | 24 |
| Robert Dingwall | 120 | 12 |
| John Lumsden | 144 | 6 |

*Source: NAS E 71/6/9: Cocket Book 14 November 1576 – 18 November 1577, fol. 3 v.-4 v.; ULStA B 10/8/6 4, 7 (two entries), 11, 14 and 16 (two entries) September 1576.*

Table 5.    Herring (in barrels) declared at Dundee by residents of Crail 1567, 1574-5 and 1577-1578/9

| | | |
|---|---|---|
| 1567 | Walter Hay | 6 |
| | Patrick Lindsay | 81 (a) |
| | John Lumsden | 7 |
| | George Meldrum | 30 |
| 1574-5 | James Annell | 132 |
| | William Annell | 48 |
| | Robert Davidson | 216 |
| 1577-1578/9 | William Annand | 6 |

a) Nine barrels on his own, 144 with Alexander Ramsay of Dundee.

*Source: NAS E 71/12/7-9.*


Table 6.    Herring declared at Edinburgh 1575/6, 1578-81, 1589-90 (barrels)

| | | |
|---|---|---|
| 1575-6 | John Wemyss, Edinburgh | 63 |
| 1578-9 (a) | John Arnot | 6 |
| | John Dougall, Edinburgh | 6 |
| | James Somerville, Edinburgh | 96 |
| 1579-80 (a) | John MacMorran, Edinburgh | 30 |
| | James Sydserf, Edinburgh | 123 |
| | John Wemyss, Edinburgh | 144 |
| 1580-1 | William Annand | 48 |
| | James Somerville, Edinburgh with Thomas Paterson, Anstruther | 108 |
| 1589-90 | Andro Bikarton | 54 |

a) These accounts do not distinguish between herring and codling.

*Source: NAS E 71/30/19-22 and E 71/32/9-10.*

Table 7.    Herring declared at Crail, Dundee and Edinburgh (barrels)

|  | Crail | Dundee | Edinburgh |
|---|---|---|---|
| 1557 | 739 | - | - |
| 1566 | 2,427 | - | - |
| 1567 | - | 124 | - |
| 1570-2 | 3,959 | - | - |
| 1573-5 | 2,335 | - | - |
| March-November 1574 | 651 | - | - |
| 1574-5 | 4,121 | 386 | - |
| 1575-6 | - | - | 63 |
| 1576-7 | 5,405 | - | - |
| 1577-1578/9 | - | 6 | - |
| 1578-9 | - | - | 108 |
| 1579-80 | - | - | 297 |
| 1580-1 |  |  | 156 (a) |
| 1582 | 2,604 | - | - |
| 1589-90 | - | - | 54 |

a) 108 barrels in joint venture between James Somerville, Edinburgh and Thomas Paterson, Anstruther.

*Source: Tables 3, 5 and 6*

Table 8.   Estimates of the value of a last of herring 1567-74, 1576-7, 1579, 1581-4, 1589-1590 (£Scots)

|  | Average value | Corrected average value |  |
|---|---|---|---|
| 1567 | 28-0-0 | - | N = 1 |
| 1568 | 24-0-0 | - | N = 2 |
| 1569 | 25-8-0 | - | N = 17 |
| 1570 | 26-1-8 | 27-9-10 (a) | N = 11 |
| 1571 | 26-17-3 | 27-5-10 (b) | N = 24 |
| 1572 | 25-0-0 | - | N = 2 |
| 1573 | 22-15-7 | 29-3-4 (c) | N = 6 |
| 1574 | 33-16-8 | - | N = 6 |
| 1576 | 29-0-6 | 30-17-4 (d) | N = 23 |
| 1577 | 32-11-1 | - | N = 6 |
| 1579 | 40-0-0 | - | N = 1 |
| 1581 | 26-0-0 | 32-0-0 (e) | N = 5 |
| 1582 | 28-16-0 | - | N = 3 |
| 1583 | 25-14-8 | 27-9-10 (f) | N = 12 |
| 1584 | 50-0-0 | - | N = 1 |
| 1589 | 44-0-0 | - | N = 1 |
| 1590 | 44-14-9 | 43-17-9 (g) | N = 19 |

a) Without an entry 28 September (£12-0-0 . b) Without an entry 10 September (£17-0-0).
c) Without entries 6 (£10-0-0) and 10 September (£8-0-0). d) Without entries 7 September (two entries, £70-0-0 and £15-0-0 ), 11 (£46-0-0), and 15 September (£16-0-0). e) Without an entry 15 September (£2-0-0). f) Without entries 18 (£12-0-0) and 19 September (£ 17-0-0) g) Without an entry 1 September (£60-0-0).

*Source: Tables 1-9 and 12- 13.*

Table 9.    Credits furnished by Alan Cunningham of Crail in 1583

| Debtor | Date | Amount | Payment | Estimated value per last | Term of payment |
|--------|------|--------|---------|--------------------------|-----------------|
| John Davidson | 27 August | 62-0-0 | 2 lasts herring from Northern Scotland | 31-0-0 | Christmas |
| John Ellis | 10 Sept | 32-0-0 | 1 last herring from Northern Scotland | 32-0-0 | Christmas |
| Alexander Simson/John Greive | 18 Sept | 34-0-0 | 2 lasts 10 barrels herring from Northern Scotland | 12-0-0 | Christmas |
| Thomas Beane/ Edward Spens | 19 Sept | 34-0-0 | 2 lasts herring from Northern Scotland | 17-0-0 | Christmas |

*Source: ULStA B 10-8-7.*

Table 10.   The price of the charter of ships 1566/7-1576 (various years)

| Date | Destination | Price (£Scots) |
|------|-------------|----------------|
| 4 February 1566/7 | Loch Broom | 30 "lyuht mony" = less than £30 |
| 13 May 1567 | Loch Broom | 25-0-0 |
| 12 October 1569 | Northern Isles | 20-0-0 |
| 9 February 1573/4 | Northern Scotland | 32-0-0 |
| 8 September 1576 | Norway | 90-0-0 |

*Source: ULStA B 10/8/4, B 10/8/5, B 10/8/6.*

Table 11.   Loading capacities of ships entered at Dundee 1580 and 1589 (in lasts and barrels)

| | Minimum | Maximum | Average | Number |
|---|---------|---------|---------|--------|
| 1580 | 17-6 | 28-0 | 23-5 | N = 4 |
| 1589 | 9-0 | 24-0 | 16-5 | N = 16 |

*Source: Dundee Shipping Lists.*

Table 12.  Loading capacities of crears entered at Dundee 1589 (in lasts and barrels)

| Minimum | Maximum | Average | Number |
|---|---|---|---|
| 9-0 | 19-5 + 6 barrels salt | 14-0 | N = 5 |

*Source: Dundee Shipping Lists.*

Table 13.  Oatmeal, Fife fiars £Scots per boll 1567-77 and 1581-3

| | Per boll | Per peck |
|---|---|---|
| 1567 | 3-13-4 | 0-4-7 |
| 1568 | 2-0-0 | 0-2-6 |
| 1569 | 3-0-0 | 0-3-9 |
| 1570 | 3-0-0 | 0-3-9 |
| 1571 | 2-0-0 | 0-2-6 |
| 1572 | 1-18-0 | 0-2-4½ |
| 1573 | 1-16-0 | 0-2-3 |
| 1574 | 3-0-0 | 0-3-9 |
| 1575 | 4-0-0 | 0-5-0 |
| 1576 | 5-0-0 | 0-6-3 |
| 1577 | 3-3-4 | 0-3-11½ |
| - | - | - |
| 1581 | 2-13-4 | 0-3-4 |
| 1582 | 3-13-4 | 0-4-7 |
| 1583 | 4-13-4 | 0-5-10 |

*Source: Gibson, A J S and Smout, T C, Prices, Food and Wages in Scotland 1550-1780, (1995, Cambridge: Cambridge University Press) p 84, cf pp 371-5.*

Table 14.  Cost of a ship for a voyage to Northern Scotland 1567-74, 1576-7, 1581-3

**(£Scots)**

| | Charter of ship (average) | Anchorage | Oatmeal (16.8.pecks of Fife) | Total |
|---|---|---|---|---|
| 1567 | 30-0-0 | 0-3-4 | 3-17-0 | 34-0-4 |
| 1568 | 30-0-0 | 0-3-4 | 2-2-0 | 32-5-4 |
| 1569 | 30-0-0 | 0-3-4 | 3-3-0 | 33-6-4 |
| 1570 | 30-0-0 | 0-3-4 | 3-3-0 | 33-6-4 |
| 1571 | 30-0-0 | 0-3-4 | 2-2-0 | 32-5-4 |
| 1572 | 30-0-0 | 0-3-4 | 1-19-11 | 32-3-3 |
| 1573 | 30-0-0 | 0-3-4 | 1-17-10 | 32-1-2 |
| 1574 | 30-0-0 | 0-3-4 | 3-3-0 | 33-6-4 |
| - | - | - | - | - |
| 1576 | 30-0-0 | 0-3-4 | 5-5-0 | 35-8-4 |
| 1577 | 30-0-0 | 0-3-4 | 3-6-6 | 33-9-10 |
| - | - | - | - | - |
| 1581 | 30-0-0 | 0-3-4 | 2-16-0 | 32-19-4 |
| 1582 | 30-0-0 | 0-3-4 | 3-17-0 | 34-0-4 |
| 1583 | 30-0-0 | 0-3-4 | 4-18-0 | 35-1-4 |

*Source: Table 13.*

Table 15.  Production costs of a last of herring, Freeman of Crail 1568, 1570-1, 1581-3

**(£Scots)**

|  | 1568 | 1570 | 1571 | 1581 | 1582 | 1583 |
|---|---|---|---|---|---|---|
| Ship (one fifteenth) | 2-3-0 | 2-4-5 | 2-3-0 | 2-4-0 | 2-5-4 | 2-6-9 |
| Salt (small) | 3-0-0 | 3-0-0 | 3-0-0 | 3-0-0 | 3-0-0 | 3-0-0 |
| Barrels | 4-3-9 | 3-11-0 | 4-3-4 | 4-0-0 | 6-13-4 | 4-6-8 |
| Customs | 0-0-8 | 0-0-8 | 0-0-8 | 0-0-8 | 0-0-8 | 0-0-8 |
| Packaging (a) | 0-4-0 | 0-4-0 | 0-4-0 | 0-4-0 | 0-4-0 | 0-4-0 |
| Packaging duty | - | - | - | 1-0-0 | 1-0-0 | 1-0-0 |
| Supplementary duty | - | - | - | - | 0-6-8 | 0-6-8 |
| Total | 9-11-5 | 9-0-1 | 9-11-0 | 10-8-8 | 13-10-0 | 11-4-9 |

a) Figure 1582-3.

*Source: Tables 2 and 14.*

Table 16.  Costs and gross profit per last of herring belonging to a Freeman of Crail 1568-1583 (various years) (£Scots)

|  | Value of last | Corrected value | Costs | Gross profit | Gross profit % |
|---|---|---|---|---|---|
| 1568 | 24-0-0 | - | 9-11-5 | 14-8-7 | 150.8 % |
| 1570 | 26-1-8 | 27-9-10 | 9-0-1 | 18-9-9 | 205.3 % |
| 1571 | 26-17-3 | 27-5-10 | 9-11-0 | 17-14-10 | 178.0 % |
| 1581 | 26-0-0 | 32-0-0 | 10-8-8 | 21-11-4 | 206.7% |
| 1582 | 28-16-0 | - | 13-10-0 | 15-6-0 | 113.3 % |
| 1583 | 25-14-8 | 27-9-10 | 11-4-9 | 16-5-1 | 144.6 % |

*Source: Tables 8 and 15.*

Table 17.  Value of a last of Scottish herring declared at the Sound Toll
(Daler pro last)

|  | Minimum | Maximum | Average |  |
|---|---|---|---|---|
| 1583 | 19 dr 0 ß | 20 dr 0 ß | 19 dr 21 1/3ß | N = 3 |
| 1589 | 30 dr 0 ß | 44 dr 0 ß | 37 dr 14 ß | N = 18 |
| 1590 | 20 dr 0 ß | 50 dr 0 ß | 36 dr 6 ß | N = 31 |

*Source: Rigsarkivet, Copenhagen. Øresundstoldregnskaber (Sound Toll Accounts) 1583, 1589 and 1590.*

Table 18.  Values of a last of Scottish herring in Daler and £Scots

|  | Sound Toll Accounts in daler | Equivalent in £Scots | Estimated value at Crail £Scots | Gross profit £Scots | Gross profit % |
|---|---|---|---|---|---|
| 1583 | 19 dr 21 1/3 ß | 38-13-4 | 27-9-10 | 11-3-6 | 40.6 % |
| 1589 | 37 dr 14 ß | 74-8-10 | 44-0-0 | 30-8-10 | 69.2% |
| 1590 | 36 dr 6 ß | 72-3-4 | 43-17-9 | 28-5-7 | 64.4 % |

*Source: Tables 16 and 17.*

Table 19.  Indemnities by the non-delivery of fish 1568, 1570-1, 1576, 1582/3, 1590 (£Scots)

| Date | Creditor | Amount advanced | Amount to pay | Indemnity | In % |
|---|---|---|---|---|---|
| 29 Sept 1568 | John Dingwall | 14-0-0 | - | - | 25 |
| do. | do. | 12-0-0 | - | - | 25 |
| 11 Sept 1570 | William Annand | 26-0-0 | 30-0-0 | 4-0-0 | 15.4 |
| 8 Sept 1571 | William Beane | 26-0-0 | 30-0-0 | 4-0-0 | 15.4 |
| 13 Sept 1571 | Patrick Lindsay | 13-0-0 | 20-0-0 | 7-0-0 | 53.9 |

| Date | Creditor | Amount advanced | Amount to pay | Indemnity | In % |
|---|---|---|---|---|---|
| 18 Sept 1576 | James Meldrum | 60-0-0 (a) | 76-0-0 | 16-0-0 | 26.7 |
| 29 Sept 1576 | Ninian Hamilton | 30-0-0 | 40-0-0 | 10-0-0 | 33.3 |
| 13 Feb 1582/3 | Steven Balfour of St Andrews | 48-0-0 | 57-0-0 | 9-0-0 | 18.75 % |
| 1 Sept 1590 | James Syd serf of Edinburgh | 60-0-0 | -(b) | 20-0-0 | 33.3 |

a) Instead of money the mariner had received 24 bolls of great (i.e. foreign) salt at 47 s. Scots the last, thus the equivalent of £ 56-8-0. b) To pay the market price plus £ 20-0-0.

*Source: ULStA B 10/8/4, B 10/8/5, B 10/8/6, B 10/8/7, and B 10/8/8.*

Table 20.  Contractors in Crail's herring fisheries

| Contractor | Date | Merchant | Barrels | Amount |
|---|---|---|---|---|
| Edward Abay | 11 Apr. 1582 | Ninian Woid | 18 | ? |
| do. | 1 June 1582 | William Morton | 12 | ? |
| do. | 22 Sept. 1590 | James Sydserf, Edinburgh | 24 | 88-0-0 |
| Thomas Abbey | 18 Sept.1577 | James Woede | 54 | ? |
| John Alexander, Cellardyke | 26 Sept.1581 | James Woid, Pittenweem | 12 | ? |
| do. | 22 Sept.1590 (a) | James Sydserf, Edinburgh | 12 | 44-0-0 |
| Robert Alexander | 4 Sept.1581 | William Morton | 3 | ? |
| do. | 7 Sept.1581 | George Martin | 12 | ? |
| do. | 18 Sept.1581 | John Melville | 9 | ? |
| do. | 23 Jan.1581/2 | George Mayerton | 3 | 11-0-0 |
| Andrew Annand | 26 May 1581 (b) | William Annand | 6 | ? |
| do. | 26 Mar. 1582 (c) | William Morton | 7 | ? |

| Contractor | Date | Merchant | Barrels | Amount |
|---|---|---|---|---|
| do. | 7 Oct. 1582 | Christine Oliphant | 24 | ? |
| William Annand | 16 Sept.1576 | William Melville | 36 | 96-0-0 |
| Walter Annell | 7 Sept. 1590 | Janet Young | 6 | 22-0-0 |
| John Arnot | 11 Sept.1571 | Patrick Lindsay | 12 | 26-0-0 |
| do. | 11 Sept.1571 (d) | do. | 18 | 39-0-0 |
| Peter Arnot, cf. John Arnot | 7 Sept. 1576 (e) | John Harte, Canongate | 24 | 60-0-0 |
| Robert Arnot, cf. Peter Arnot | 16 Sept. 1571 | Thomas Kay | 12 | 28-0-0 |
| do. | 4 Sept.1576 | Walter Ballingall | 18 | 35-0-0 |
| do. | 16 Sept.1576 | Patrick Lindsay | 12 | ? |
| do. | 18 Apr. 1577 | do. | 12 | ? |
| do. | 21 Sept. 1577 (f) | do. | 12 | ? |
| do. | 29 Apr. 1578 | John Harte, Canongate | 12 | ? |

a) With Thomas Duncan, Alexander Farmer, John Galloway younger and John Simson. b) With John Reid younger. c) With John Annand. d) With Peter Arnot. e) With Robert Arnot. f) With Steven Arnot.

| Contractor | Date | Merchant | Barrels | Amount |
|---|---|---|---|---|
| Robert Arnot, cf. Peter Arnot | 19 Sept.1578 (a) | John Harte, Canongate | 12 | ? |
| do. | 27 May 1579 | Ninian Woed | 18 | ? |
| do. | 21 Dec.1579 | Walter Ballingall | 12 | ? |
| do. | 6 Sept. 1580 | John Simson | 18 | ? |
| do. | 18 Sept.1580 | John Harte, Canongate | 12 | ? |
| do. | 6 Sept. 1581 | John Simson | 12 | ? |
| do. | 15 Sept. 1581 | Thomas Beane younger | 12 | ? |

| Contractor | Date | Merchant | Barrels | Amount |
|---|---|---|---|---|
| Steven Arnot, cf. Robert Arnot | 25 Sept. 1572 | John Spens | 12 | ? |
| do. | 7 Sept.1576 | John Harte, Canongate | 24 | 60-0-0 |
| do. | 16 Sept.1576 | Walter Ballingall | 12 | 23-6-8 |
| do. | 15 Dec.1576 | do. | 12 | ? |
| do. | 25 Sept.1580 | John Cass, West Anstruther | 12 | ? |
| do. | 30 Sept.1580 | Archibald Thomson, East Anstruther | 18 | ? |
| do. | 26 Sept.1581 (b) | Archibald Wishart, St Andrews | 18 | ? |
| do. | 12 Sept.1582 | do. | ? | ? |
| do. | 29 Apr. 1583 (c) | George Corstorphine | 1,000 fresh ling | ? |
| do. | 2 May 1583 (c) | John Hamilton, Edinburgh | 1,500 keiling | ? |
| William Arnot | 3 Sept. 1569 (d) | Alexander Arbuthnot | 12 | One chalder flour |
| do. | 23 Sept.1570 | Thomas Welwood, St Andrews | 6 | ? |
| do. | 7 Sept.1576 | John Harte, Canongate | 24 | 60-0-0 |
| do. | 20 Sept.1577 | Harry Lindsay | 24 | 40-0-0 |
| do. | 15 Oct. 1577 | Walter Ballingall | 12 | ? |
| do. | 6 May 1578 | Andro Lindsay | 6 | ? |

a) With John Bowsie. b) With Robert Dingwall. c) With George Bell, Fisherrow. d) With WilliamArnot II, John Bowsie, Patrick Geddes, William Kam and William Kay.

| Contractor | Date | Merchant | Barrels | Amount |
|---|---|---|---|---|
| William Arnot | 16 Sept.1579 | Margaret Gowan | 12 + 8 | 20-0-0 |
| John Arrock | 17 May 1576 | Margaret Cornwall | 12 | ? |
| Robert Arrock | 4 Sept. 1573 | Patrick Lindsay | 12 | 35-0-0 |
| John Auld | 15 Sept. 1569 | Henry Aymour | 6 | ? |
| John Balcony | 30 Aug. 1580 | William Morton | 12 | ? |
| do. | 8 Sept.1580 | John Simson | 18 | ? |
| do. | 27 Febr. 1581/2 | William Morton | 12 | ? |
| do. | 3 Sept.1582 | do. | 18 | ? |
| Robert Balcony | 1 Apr. 1572 | ? | 168 | ? |
| Robert Ballie | 26 May 1579 | Ninian Hamilton | 12 | 22-0-0 |
| Andro Baxter | 7 Sept. 1571 | Patrick Dyk | 12 | 28-0-0 |
| do. | 16 Sept.1571 | Thomas Kay | 6 | 14-0-0 |
| do. | 18 Sept. 1572 | Patrick Lindsay | 12 | 26-0-0 |
| do. | 26 Sept.1572 | do. | 1 | ? |
| do. | 6 Sept. 1573 | do. | 12 | 12-0-0 |
| do. | 10 Sept.1573 | do. | 6 | 4-0-0 |
| do. | 18 Sept.1573 | do. | 7 | ? |
| Thomas Beane | 28 Aug.1576 | Ninian Hamilton | 18 | ? |
| do. | 9 May 1582 (a) | John Melville | 12 | ? |
| do. | 20 Sept.1582 (b) | Alan Cunningham | 36 | ? |
| do. | 19 Sept.1583 | do. | 24 | 34-0-0 |
| Alexander Bikarton | 29 Sept.1568 | John Dingwall | 6 | 12-0-0 |
| do. | 29 Sept. 1569 | do. | 6 | 8-13-4 |
| do. | 27 Sept.1570 | Patrick Lindsay | 12 | ? |
| Andro Bikarton | 11 Aug. 1569 (c) | William Annand | 42 | 84-0-0 |
| do. | 20 Sept.1569 | do. | 2 | 4-6-8 |

| Contractor | Date | Merchant | Barrels | Amount |
|---|---|---|---|---|
| do. | 27 Sept.1570 | Patrick Lindsay | 12 | ? |
| do. | 24 Sept.1572 | do. | 36? (d) | 72-0-0 |
| do. | 27 Aug. 1574 | Walter Ballingall | 12 | ? |

a) With William Bowsie. b) With Thomas Blair. c) With George Corstorphine and Thomas Martin. d) Ms. 3; the amount £72-0-0 appears excessive, if barrels and not lasts are meant.

| Contractor | Date | Merchant | Barrels | Amount |
|---|---|---|---|---|
| Andro Bikarton | 26 Aug. 1576 | John Harte, Canongate | 12 | ? |
| do. | 7 Sept. 1576 | Walter Ballingall | 6 | 35-0-0 |
| do. | 9 Sept. 1576 | Patrick Lindsay | 6 | ? |
| do. | 11 Sept. 1576 | William Annand | 12 | 36-0-0 |
| Thomas Blair, cf. Thomas Beane | 14 Sept. 1580 | William Morton | 24 | ? |
| do. | 15 Sept.1580 (a) | do. | 12 | ? |
| do. | 8 Sept. 1583 | John Dougall | 24 | 23-6-8 |
| John Bowsie, cf. Robert Arnot, William Arnot | 19 Oct.1569 (b) | Robert Constable, Wellington | 18 | 54-0-0 |
| do. | 20 Oct.1569 (b) | do. | 24 | 72-0-0 |
| do. | 8 Sept.1571 | Alexander Reid, Prestonpans | 21 | 49-0-0 |
| William Bowsie, cf. ThomasBeane | 10 Sept.1582 | John Simson younger | 20 | 34-0-0 |
| do. | 12 Sept.1582 (c) | Archibald Wishart | 6 | ? |
| James Brownie, West Anstruther | 26 Aug.1581 | Ninian Woede | 6 | ? |
| John Brownie | 7 Sept.1582 (d) | John MacMoran, Edinburgh | 18 | 51-0-0 |
| John Bruce | 6 Sept.1577 (d) | Patrick Lindsay | 6 | ? |

| Contractor | Date | Merchant | Barrels | Amount |
|---|---|---|---|---|
| do. | 14 Sept.1581 | William Morton | 2 | ? |
| do. | 18 Sept. 1581 | John Melville | 12 | ? |
| do. | 21 Apr.1582 | do. | 6 | ? |
| do. | 21 Sept. 1582 | Alan Cunningham | 6 | ? |
| John Burgess | 5 Sept. 1577 | William Hawson | 9? | ? |
| William Burgess | 15 Sept.1569 | John Dingwall | 12 | ? |
| do. | 23 Sept.1571 | Patrick Lindsay | 1 | 3-0-0 |
| John "Caddowy", Anstruther | 29 Sept.1576 | Ninian Hamilton | 12 | 30-0-0 |
| Andro Calvert | 4 Sept.1569 | William Annand | 12 | 24-0-0 |
| John Calvert | 6 Sept.1580 | John Simson | 24 | ? |

a) With John Corstorphine younger. b) With William Kay. c) With Andro Fuirde.
d) With Arthur Gray.

| Contractor | Date | Merchant | Barrels | Amount |
|---|---|---|---|---|
| James Cass | 7 Sept. 1576 (a) | Patrick Hogg, Kirkcaldy | 36 | 32-0-0 |
| do. | 21 Sept. 1576 (a) | Walter Ballingall | 12 | ? |
| do. | 30 Sept. 1578 | Patrick Lindsay | 21 | ? |
| Andro Corstorphine | 27 Aug. 1569 | William Annand | 12 | 24-0-0 |
| do. | 27 Sept. 1569 | George Meldrum | 6 | 12-0-0 |
| do. | 12 Sept. 1570 (b) | Thomas Hall, Prestonpans | 24 | 28-0-0 |
| do. | 23 Sept. 1570 (b) | Patrick Lindsay | 10 | 25-0-0 |
| George Corstorphine, cf. Andro Bikarton | 7 Sept. 1569 | George Christie, Dysart | 12 | 13-0-0 |

| Contractor | Date | Merchant | Barrels | Amount |
|---|---|---|---|---|
| do. | 1 Sept. 1571 | James Monipenny | 9 | 20-0-0 |
| do. | 7 Sept. 1576 | John Harte, Canongate | 12 | 30-0-0 |
| do. | 15 Sept. 1576 | William Corstorphine elder | 12 | 16-0-0 |
| James Corstorphine | 14 Sept. 1576 | William Morton | 6 | 15-10-0 |
| do. | 3 Sept. 1577 | do. | 12 | ? |
| do. | 22 Sept. 1590 | James Sydserth, Edinburgh | 9 | 33-15-0 |
| John Corstorphine elder | 27 Sept. 1570 | Patrick Lindsay | 12 | ? |
| do. | 25 Sept.1580 (c) | John Harte, Canongate | 6 | ? |
| John Corstorphine younger, cf. Thomas Blair | 5 Sept. 1590 (d) | Thomas Blair | 12 | ? |
| John Craig | 2 Oct. 1555 | William Bowsie | 1 barrel keiling + 1 barrel "gvd-lingis" | ? |
| William Culiwark | 12 May 1574 | William Powsta | 1 dozen dry fish | 18-10-0 |
| David Currour | 22 Jan. 1567/8 | Andrew Peirson | ? | ? |
| William Currour | 26 Aug. 1577 | David Page, Cupar | 12 | ? |
| do. | 8 Sept.1577 | Patrick Lindsay | 9 | 8-0-0 |
| Andro Davidson elder | 7 Sept.1577 | William Annand, landman | 18 | ? |
| do. | 7 May 1590 | Duncan Balfour, St Andrews | 12 | 45-0-0 |

a) With James Dingwall and John Martin. b) With Andro Peirson c) With John Mayerton. d) With Roland Laverock and John Martin.

| Contractor | Date | Merchant | Barrels | Amount |
|---|---|---|---|---|
| Andro Davidson younger | 1 Sept.1590 | Thomas Myrton | 9 | 30-0-0 |
| do. | 1 Sept. 1590 | James Sydserf, Edinburgh | 12 | 60-0-0 |
| do. | 13 Sept.1590 | David Grig, St Andrews | 13 | ? |
| do. | 20 Sept. 1590 | Ninian Wode | 12 | 44-0-0 |
| do. | 28 Sept. 1590 | John Melville | 9 | 30-0-0 |
| George Davidson | 23 Sept. 1567 | John Lumsden | 12 | 28-0-0 |
| do. | 3 Sept. 1569 | Alexander Reid, Prestonpans | 12 | 26-0-0 |
| John Davidson | 17 June 1572 | James Nicoll, Edinburgh | 168 | ? |
| do. | 17 June 1572 | ? | 72 | ? |
| do. | 21 Apr. 1582 | John Melville | 6 | ? |
| do. | 3 Sept. 1582 | Alan Cunningham | 6 | ? |
| do. | 9 Sept. 1582 | John Black, St Andrews | 6 | ? |
| do. | 27 Aug. 1583 | Alan Cunningham | 24 | 62-0-0 |
| Thomas Davidson younger | 24 Nov. 1579 | George Meldrum | 18 | ? |
| William Davidson | 7 Sept. 1569 | George Christie, Dysart | 24 | ? |
| do. | 9 Sept. 1569 | William Annand | 6 | 12-0-0 |
| do. | 25 Sept.1569 | do. | 1 | 2-0-0 |
| do. | 9 Sept.1574 | Nicol Uddart, Edinburgh | 18 | 48-0-0 |
| do. | 22 Sept. 1574 | David Beane | 18 | 43-10-0 |
| Andro Daw, Largo | 27 Aug.1582 | Edward Grig | 6 | ? |

| Contractor | Date | Merchant | Barrels | Amount |
|---|---|---|---|---|
| William Daw | 24 Sept.1577 | William Morton, cooper | 6 | ? |
| do. | 12 Sept.1589 | William Monipenny | 48 | 176-0-0 |
| John Dawson | 25 Sept.1570 | William Stirling, Edinburgh | 30 | 67-10-0 |
| do. | 7 Sept.1576 | Patrick Hogg, Kirkcaldy | 36 | 96-0-0 |
| do. | 21 Sept. 1576 | John Davidson, baxter | 12 | ? |
| do. | 23 Sept. 1576 | William Spens | 6 | ? |
| do. | 4 Oct. 1577 | Patrick Hogg, Kirkcaldy | 36 | 135-0-0 |
| Robert Dawson | 3 Sept. 1576 | Thomas Martin | 18 | 45-0-0 |
| do. | 9 Sept.1576 | John Harte, Canongate | 12 | ? |
| Thomas Dawson | 13 Sept.1590 | William Powstey, Cellardyke | 100 herring + 4 salt fish keiling | 45-0-0 |
| William Dawson | 17 Sept. 1583 | John Welwood, St Andrews | 6 | ? |
| James Dingwall, cf. James Cass | 7 Sept. 1569 | George Christie, Dysart | 12 | 13-0-0 |
| Robert Dingwall, cf. Steven Arnot | 14 Sept. 1576 | William Melville | 12 | 32-0-0 |
| do. | 20 Sept. 1579 | Archibald Wishart St Andrews | 12 | ? |
| do. | 6 May 1580 | Patrick Hogg, Kirkcaldy | 12 | ? |
| do. | 10 Sept. 1580 | Patrick Littlejohn, St Andrews | 6 | ? |

| Contractor | Date | Merchant | Barrels | Amount |
|---|---|---|---|---|
| do. | 21 Sept.1580 | William Lyall | 6 | ? |
| do. | 18 Apr. 1581 | Archibald Kay | 2 | 6-0-0 |
| do. | 25 Sept. 1581 | James Woide | 12 | ? |
| do. | 21 Sept.1582 | Edward Grig | 6 | ? |
| do. | 17 Sept.1583 | James Geddy | 12 | ? |
| John Dowekand | 4 Sept.1570 | William Annand | 12 | 26-0-0 |
| Patrick Dyk | 25 Sept.1580 | John Harte, Canongate | 6 | ? |
| do. | 2 Sept. 1581 | John Traille, Dundee | 12 | ? |
| John Edyson | 6 Sept. 1583 | Robert Fyndlayson Dundee | 6 | 10-0-0 |
| John Ellis | 10 Sept.1583 | Alan Cunningham | 12 | 32-0-0 |
| Alexander Farmer, cf. John Alexander | 27 Sept.1569 | Alexander Airth, Thomas Kay | 12 | 25-0-0 |
| do. | 10 Sept.1571 | Alexander Reid, Prestonpans | 12 | 17-0-0 |
| do. | 13 Sept.1571 | William Annand | 6 | 13-0-0 |
| do. | 18 Sept.1571 | do. | 2 | ? |
| do. | 2 Sept. 1573 | John Melville | 24 | 58-0-0 |
| do. | 19 Sept.1576 | William Melville | 36 | 96-0-0 |
| do. | 21 Sept. 1577 | Ninian Woede | 18 | ? |
| do. | 25 Sept.1580 | John Harte, Canongate | 18 | ? |
| do. | 4 Oct. 1580 | Ninian Woede | 12 | ? |
| do. | 13 Sept.1581 | do. | 42 | ? |
| do. | 15 Sept.1590 | John Melville | 6 | ? |
| do. | 18 Sept.1590 | James Sydserf, Edinburgh | 18 | 66-0-0 |
| do. | 22 Sept.1590 | Ninian Woede | 6 1/2 | 23-16-8 |

| Contractor | Date | Merchant | Barrels | Amount |
|---|---|---|---|---|
| John Gardiner | 15 Sept. 1569 | John Dingwall | 36 | ? |
| do. | 12 Sept.1576 | William Annand | 6 | 17-0-0 |
| Patrick Geddes, cf. William Arnot | 21 Aug. 1570 | Alexander Reid, Prestonpans | 6 | ? |
| William Gilbert | 29 Sept.1569 | John Dingwall | 12 | 17-6-8 |
| do. | 7 Sept. 1570 | William Bowsie younger | 12 | 25-0-0 |
| do. | 16 Sept.1571 | David Beane | 12 | 27-0-0 |
| do. | 22 Sept.1571 | Thomas Clark | 6 | 14-10-0 |
| do. | 18 Sept.1572 | David Beane | 18 | 39-0-0 |
| George Gilruth | 28 Sept.1590 | Androw Clark | 6 | 22-0-0 |
| John Gilruth | 22 Sept.1590 | James Sydserth, Edinburgh | 6 | 22-10-0 |
| William Grahamslaw | 6 Sept.1583 | Androw Blyt | 12 | 34-0-0 |
| Arthur Gray, cf. John Brownie, John Bruce | 15 Sept.1570 | William Annand | 12 | 26-0-0 |
| do. | 16 Sept.1571 | Thomas Clark | 12 | 26-0-0 |
| do. | 7 Sept.1576 | Margaret Cornwall | 18 | 46-0-0 |
| do. | 12 Sept.1576 | William Melville | 12 | 32-0-0 |
| do. | 20 Apr. 1577 | Patrick Lindsay | 12 | ? |
| do. | 9 Sept. 1577 | Margaret Cornwall | 18 | ? |
| do. | 16 Sept.1577 | Andro Lindsay | 6 | 23-6-8 |
| do. | 30 Nov. 1577 | Patrick Lindsay | 12 | 42-0-0 |
| do. | 19 Nov.1579 | William Hunter | 16 | ? |
| do. | 6 May 1580 | Patrick Hogg, Kirkcaldy | 6 | ? |
| do. | 21 Mar. 1580/1 | William Morton | 12 | ? |

| Contractor | Date | Merchant | Barrels | Amount |
|---|---|---|---|---|
| do. | 18 Apr. 1581 | James Woid | 12 | ? |
| do. | 30 Aug. 1581 | John Harte, Canongate | 12 | ? |
| do. | 30 Aug. 1581 | John Harte, Canongate | 12 | ? |
| do. | 2 Sept. 1581 | James Summerville, Edinburgh | 24 | ? |
| do. | 17 Nov. 1581 | John Summerville, Edinburgh | 24 | 60-0-0 |
| do. | 19 Nov. 1581 (a) | John Harte, Canongate | 24 | 60-0-0 |
| do. | 22 Nov. 1581 | Edward Grig | 6 | ? |
| do. | 26 Mar. 1582 | William Morton | 12 | ? |
| do. | 3 Sept. 1582 | Alan Cunningham | 12 | ? |
| do. | 13 Sept. 1582 | Ninian Woede | 78 | ? |
| do. | 13 Febr. 1582/3 | Steven Balfour, St Andrews | 18 | 57-0-0 |
| do. | 3 Dec. 1583 | James Woid | 18 | 33-15-0 |
| John Gray | 30 Aug. 1580 | John Welwood, St Andrews | 12 | ? |
| Robert Gray | 13 Oct. 1555 (b) | William Kay | 15,000 herring | ? |
| John Greif? | 14 Sept. 1569 | William Annand | 6 | ? |
| do. | 8 Sept. 1571 | William Beane | 12 | 26-0-0 |
| do. | 18 Sept. 1572 | David Beane | 12 | 26-0-0 |
| do. | 11 Sept.1573 | William Beane | 18 | 39-0-0 ? |
| do. | 2 Sept.1574 | Ninian Hamilton | 6 | 23-0-0 |
| do. | 7 Sept.1576 | do. | 6 | 6-0-0 |
| do. | 18 Sept.1583 | Alan Cunningham | 14 | 14-0-0 |

a) With John Paterson. b) With William Gray.

| Contractor | Date | Merchant | Barrels | Amount |
|---|---|---|---|---|
| David Hawson | 29 Sept.1568 | John Dingwall | 7 | 14-0-0 |
| William Hawson | 16 Sept.1571 | John Reid | 6 | ? |
| do. | 17 Sept.1571 | William Annand | 6 | 13-0-0 |
| do. | 30 Aug. 1576 | do. | 6 | 16-5-0 |
| do. | 14 Sept. 1576 | James Meldrum | 18 | ? |
| do. | 29 Mar. 1580 | James Woed | 12 | ? |
| William Hunter | 25 Aug. 1590 | William Currour, Simon Spens | 66 | ? |
| John Kay | 10 Sept.1574 | Nicol Uddart, Edinburgh | 7 | 18-13-4 |
| William Kay, cf. William Arnot, John Bowsie | 11 Febr. 1566/7 | William Birnie, Edinburgh | 24 | ? |
| do. | 12 Sept. 1570 (a) | Alexander Reid, Prestonpans | 42 | 96-5-0 |
| do. | 16 Sept.1570 | John Wemyss, Edinburgh | 12 | 28-0-0 |
| do. | 21 Sept. 1574 | Nicol Uddart, Edinburgh | 12 | 32-0-0 |
| do. | 30 Aug. 1581 | John Harte, Canongate | 12 | ? |
| do. | 19 Aug.1582 | Thomas Farmer | 12 | ? |
| George Kid | 26 Sept. 1569 | John Dingwall | 12 | ? |
| Robert King | 26 Aug. 1577 | David Page, Cupar | 12 | ? |
| Robert King younger | 3 Sept. 1580 | James Summerville, Edinburgh | 8 | ? |
| Alexander Kinnaird | 14 Sept.1580 | William Morton | 12 | ? |
| do. | 14 Sept.1581 | do. | 12 | ? |
| do. | 30 Dec.1581 | do. | 12 | ? |

| Contractor | Date | Merchant | Barrels | Amount |
|---|---|---|---|---|
| do. | 6 Sept.1583 | Robert Fyndlayson, Dundee | 12 | 20-0-0 |
| Thomas Kinninmonth | 5 Sept.1577 | William Hawson | 9 | ? |
| do. | 14 Sept.1580 | John Harte, Canongate | 12 | ? |

a) With Thomas Martin.

| Contractor | Date | Merchant | Barrels | Amount |
|---|---|---|---|---|
| Alexander Laverock | 4 Sept.1571 | Helen Bethell | 12 | 27-0-0 |
| Roland Laverock | 5 Sept.1580 (a) | Thomas Blair | 12 | ? |
| Andrew Lonye | 22 Sept.1590 | James Sydserf, Edinburgh | 6 | 22-10-0 |
| JohnLumsden | 11 Sept.1576 | William Corstorphine elder | 6 | 23-0-0 |
| William Lyall | 15 Sept.1580 | John Simson younger | 24 | ? |
| do. | 2 Sept.1581 | John Traille, Dundee | 24 | 68-0-0 |
| do. | 3 Sept.1583 | David Belland younger, Cupar | 12 | 30-0-0 |
| do. | 8 Sept.1583 | John Fyschars | 12 | 36-0-0 |
| do. | 8 Sept.1583 | James Geddy | 48 | ? |
| James Martin | 26 Aug. 1576 | John Harte, Canongate | 12 | ? |
| do. | 4 Sept. 1576 | do. | 12 | ? |
| John Martin, cf. James Cass, John Corstorphine younger, Roland Laverock | 12 Sept. 1581 | John Dougall, younger, Edinburgh | 12 | ? |

| Contractor | Date | Merchant | Barrels | Amount |
|---|---|---|---|---|
| do. | 13 Sept. 1581 | William Morton | 12 | ? |
| do. | 8 Sept. 1583 | John Dougall | 12 | 11-13-4 |
| do. | 30 Mar. 1584 (b) | John Summerville, Edinburgh | 12 | ? |
| do. | 28 Sept. 1590 | Janet Young | 6 | 22-10-0 |
| Thomas Martin, cf. Andro Bikarton, William Kay | 14 Oct. 1569 | George Meldrum | 12 | 24-0-0 |
| do. | 10 Sept. 1571 | Alexander Reid, Prestonpans | 12 | 28-0-0 |
| do. | 26 Aug. 1576 | John Harte, Canongate | 18 | ? |
| do. | 8 Sept. 1576 | Walter Ballingall | 18 | ? |
| William Martin | 12 July 1590 (c) | James Williamson | ? | 220-0-0 |
| Thomas Mayerton | 16 Sept. 1580 | John Harte, Canongate | 12 | ? |

a) With John Martin. b) With Edward Spens. c) With Robert Morris and John Parkie.

| Contractor | Date | Merchant | Barrels | Amount |
|---|---|---|---|---|
| Andro Melville, Anstruther | 27 May 1578 | John Melville | 14 | 43-3-4 |
| John Melville | 16 Sept. 1570 | John Wemyss, Edinburgh | 12 | 28-0-0 |
| John Melville Younger | 17 Sept. 1579 | Andrew Melville younger, Anstruther | 12 | ? |
| do. | 30 Apr. 1582 | Robert Blackburn, Rouen | 54 (a) | ? |
| do. | 19 Sept. 1582 | Alan Cunningham | 24 | ? |
| Robert Morris, cf William Martin | 12 May 1580 | William Morton | 1 | ? |

| Contractor | Date | Merchant | Barrels | Amount |
|---|---|---|---|---|
| Thomas Morris | 20 Sept. 1573 | Alexander Farmer | 6 | ? |
| do. | 10 Sept. 1574 | Nicol Uddart, Edinburgh | 6 | 16-0-0 |
| do. | 5 Sept.1577 | William Hawson | 1 | ? |
| Thomas Morrison | 28 Sept. 1570 | Patrick Lindsay | 1 | 1-0-0 |
| Robert Muyr | 23 Sept. 1566 | Charles Watson | 2 | ? |
| William "Obondis" | 20 Sept. 1569 | John Ramsay | 2 | 4-6-8 |
| John Ottar | 17 Sept. 1577 | William Morton, cooper | 12 | ? |
| Robert Ottar | 1 Sept. 1577 | William Morton, cooper | 12 | 31-0-0 |
| do. | 18 Sept. 1577 | Ninian Woede | 12 | ? |
| John Paterson, cf. Arthur Gray | 12 June 1581 | Thomas Welwood, St Andrews | 12 | ? |
| do. | 12 Sept.1582 | John Melville | 12 | ? |
| Thomas Patie, younger | 1 June 1582 | John Melville | 6 | ? |
| Andro Payson | 14 Sept. 1569 | William Annand | 12 | ? |
| George Peirson | 7 Sept. 1576 | Patrick Hogg, Kirkcaldy | 24 | 64-0-0 |
| do. | 12 Sept.1576 | William Corstorphine elder | 12 | ? |
| do. | 12 Sept.1576 | James Meldrum | 24 | ? |
| do. | 12 Sept.1581 | John Dougall, younger, Edinburgh | 24 | ? |

a) 27 barrels by 2 Febr.1582/3 and 27 by 2 Febr. 1583/4.

| Contractor | Date | Merchant | Barrels | Amount |
|---|---|---|---|---|
| George Peirson | 20 Sept.1590 | Ninian Woid | 12 | 44-0-0 |
| Alexander Reid | 12 Sept.1576 | John Harte, Canongate | 6 | ? |
| John Reid elder | 10 Sept.1571 | Alexander Reid, Prestonpans | 24 | 56-0-0 |
| do. | 29 Mar. 1581 | Ninian Woed | 24 | ? |
| do. | 11 Sept.1581 | John Dougall younger, Edinburgh | 18 | ? |
| do. | 8 Jan. 1581/2 | William Annand | 6 | 16-0-0 |
| Thomas Robertson | 7 Febr. 1582/3 | James Summerville, Edinburgh | 6 barrels keiling | ? |
| William Robertson | 24 Sept.1582 | John Harte, Canongate | 12 | ? |
| David Scott | 18 Sept.1576 | James Meldrum | 24 | 60-0-0 |
| John Selkirk | 15 Sept.1590 | Janet Young | 6 | 22-0-0 |
| Alexander Simson | 21 Sept.1582 | Alan Cunningham | 12 | ? |
| do. | 18 Sept.1583 | do. | 20 | 20-0-0 |
| John Simson, cf. John Alexander | 22 Sept.1590 | James Sydserf, Edinburgh | 6 | 22-0-0 |
| Thomas Simson | 13 Sept.1576 | Patrick Lindsay | 12 | ? |
| do. | 26 Aug. 1577 | David Page, Cupar | 12 | ? |
| do. | 17 Sept.1577 | Patrick Lindsay | 12 | ? |
| John Smith | 16 Sept.1571 | David Beane | 12 | 28-0-0 |
| do. | 31 May 1576 | Patrick Lindsay | 12 | ? |
| do. | 25 Sept.1581 | James Woid | 18 | ? |
| do. | 7 Sept. 1582 | John MacMoran, Edinburgh | 24 | 68-0-0 |
| do. | 7 Oct.1582 | Christine Oliphant | 24 | ? |

| Contractor | Date | Merchant | Barrels | Amount |
|---|---|---|---|---|
| William Smith, cooper | 12 Apr. 1580 | William Morton | 2 | ? |
| do. | 3 Sept.1581 | do. | 1 | ? |
| Edward Spens, cf. John Martin | 19 Sept.1583 | Alan Cunningham | 6 | 8-10-0 |
| do. | 7 Febr.1583/4 | William Spens | 14 | ? |
| John Spens | 30 Aug. 1577 | John Lindsay, Cupar | 12 | ? |
| Andro Stevenson | 3 Sept.1577 | David Logemonthe | 12 | ? |
| Alexander Wemyss | 28 Aug. 1576 | John Holbetar (?) | 12 | ? |
| Harry White | 2 Sept.1581 | John Traille, Dundee | 12 | 34-0-0 |
| Andro Wilson | 9 Sept.1571 | William Annand | 6 | 13-0-0 |
| do. | 23 Sept.1571 | Edward Grig | 6 | 13-0-0 |
| do. | 23 Sept.1571 | Thomas Kay | 3 | 6-10-0 |
| John Wilson, huikmaker | 1 June 1582 | William Morton | 6 | ? |
| John Wilson, seaman | 8 Sept.1582 | George Martin | 12 | 32-0-0 |
| do. | 14 Sept.1583 | do. | 18 | 46-0-0 |
| John Wilson | 25 Sept.1580 | Alexander Farmer | 6 | ? |
| do. | 13 Sept.1581 | George Mayerton | 12 | ? |
| do. | 14 Sept.1581 | Ninian Woid | 18 | ? |
| John Witkow | 22 Sept.1590 | James Sydserth, Edinburgh | 12 | 45-0-0 |
| Alexander Woede | 6 Oct.1570 | Patrick Lindsay | 5 | 12-5-0 |
| do. | 13 Sept.1571 | Patrick Lindsay | 6 | 13-0-0 |
| do. | 4 Sept.1576 | John Harte, Canongate | 12 | ? |
| do. | 9 Sept.1577 | William Morton, cooper | 18 | ? |

| Contractor | Date | Merchant | Barrels | Amount |
|---|---|---|---|---|
| William Woed | 14 Sept.1577 | Walter Ballingall | 24 | ? |
| William Young | 15 Sept.1569 | George Meldrum | 24 | 49-0-0 |
| do. | 23 Sept.1571 | David Beane | 14 | 19-0-0 |

Table 21. Obligations by contractors

| Merchant | Date | Contractor | Barrels | £Scots |
|---|---|---|---|---|
| Alexander Airth with Thomas Kay | 27 Sept.1569 | Alexander Farmer | 12 | 25-0-0 |
| William Annand, landman | 7 Sept. 1577 | Andro Davidson | 18 | ? |
| William Annand, merchant | 11 Aug. 1569 | Andro Bikarton, George Corstorphine Thomas Martin | 42 | 84-0-0 |
| do. | 27 Aug. 1569 | Andro Corstorphine | 12 | 24-0-0 |
| do. | 4 Sept. 1569 | Andro Calvert | 12 | 24-0-0 |
| do. | 9 Sept. 1569 | William Davidson | 6 | 12-0-0 |
| do. | 14 Sept. 1569 | Andro Bikarton, John Greif, Andro Payson | 18 | ? |
| do. | 20 Sept.1569 | Andro Bikarton | 2 | 4-6-8 |
| do. | 25 Sept. 1569 | William Davidson | 1 | 2-0-0 |
| do. | 4 Sept. 1570 | John "Dovekand" | 12 | 26-0-0 |
| do. | 9 Sept. 1571 | Andro Wilson | 6 | 13-0-0 |
| do. | 13 Sept. 1571 | Alexander Farmer | 6 | 13-0-0 |
| do. | 17 Sept. 1571 | William Hawson | 6 | 13-0-0 |

| Merchant | Date | Contractor | Barrels | £Scots |
|---|---|---|---|---|
| do. | 18 Sept. 1571 | Alexander Farmer | 2 | ? |
| do. | 30 Aug. 1576 | William Hawson | 6 | 16-5-0 |
| do. | 11 Sept. 1576 | Andro Bikarton | 12 | 36-0-0 |
| do. | 12 Sept. 1576 | John Gardiner | 6 | 17-0-0 |
| do. | 26 May 1581 | Androw Annand, John Reid, younger | 6 | ? |
| do. | 8 Jan.1581/2 | John Reid elder | 6 | 16-0-0 |
| William Annell | 15 Sept. 1570 | Arthur Gray | 12 | 26-0-0 |
| Alexander Arbuthnot, Edinburgh | 3 Sept. 1569 | William Arnot I and II, John Bowsie, Patrick Geddes, William Kam, William Kay | 12 | One chalder flour |
| Henry Aymour | 15 Sept. 1569 | John Auld | 6 | ? |
| Duncan Balfour, St Andrews | 7 May 1590 | Andro Davidson elder | 12 | 45-0-0 |
| Steven Balfour, St Andrews | 13 Febr. 1582/3 | Arthur Gray | 18 | 57-0-0 |
| Walter Ballingall | 27 Aug. 1574 | Andro Bikarton | 12 | ? |
| do. | 4 Sept. 1576 | Robert Arnot | 18 | 35-0-0 |
| do. | 7 Sept. 1576 | Andro Bikarton | 6 | 35-0-0 |
| do. | 8 Sept. 1576 | Thomas Martin | 18 | ? |
| do. | 16 Sept. 1576 | Steven Arnot | 12 | 23-6-8 |
| do. | 21 Sept. 1576 | James Cass, James Dingwall, John Martin | 12 | ? |
| do. | 15 Dec. 1576 | Steven Arnot | 12 | ? |
| do. | 14 Sept. 1577 | William Woed | 24 | ? |
| do. | 15 Oct. 1577 | William Arnot | 12 | ? |

| Merchant | Date | Contractor | Barrels | £Scots |
|---|---|---|---|---|
| do. | 21 Dec. 1579 | Robert Arnot | 12 | 30-0-0 |
| David Beane | 16 Sept. 1571 | William Gilbert | 12 | 27-0-0 |
| do. | 16 Sept. 1571 | John Smith | 12 | 28-0-0 |
| do. | 23 Sept. 1571 | William Young | 14 | 19-0-0 |
| do. | 18 Sept. 1572 | William Gilbert | 18 | 39-0-0 |
| do. | 18 Sept. 1572 | John Greif | 12 | 26-0-0 |
| do. | 22 Sept. 1574 | William Davidson | 18 | 43-10-0 |
| Thomas Beane younger | 15 Sept. 1581 | Robert Arnot | 12 | ? |
| William Beane | 8 Sept. 1571 | John Greif | 12 | 26-0-0 |
| do. | 11 Sept. 1573 | do. | 18 | 39-0-0 |
| David Belland younger, Cupar | 3 Sept. 1583 | William Lyall | 12 | 30-0-0 |
| Helen Bethell, John Dingwall's widow | 4 Sept. 1571 | Alexander Laverock | 12 | 27-0-0 |
| William Birnie, Edinburgh | 11 Febr. 1566/7 | William Kay | 24 | ? |
| John Black, St Andrews | 9 Sept. 1582 | John Davidson | 6 | ? |
| Robert Blackburn, Rouen | 30 Apr. 1582 | John Melville | 27 to deliver by 2 Feb 1582/3, 27 to deliver one year later | 40-0-0 per 12 barrels |
| Thomas Blair | 5 Sept. 1580 | John Corstorphine younger, John Martin | 12 | ? |

| Merchant | Date | Contractor | Barrels | £Scots |
|---|---|---|---|---|
| do. | 5 Sept. 1580 | Roland Laverock, John Martin | 12 | ? |
| Andrew Blyt | 6 Sept. 1583 | William Grahamslaw | 12 | 34-0-0 |
| William Bowsie | 2 Oct. 1555 | John Craig | 1 barrel keiling, 1 barrel gvdlyngis | ? |
| William Bowsie younger | 7 Sept. 1570 | William Gilbert | 12 | 25-0-0 |
| John Cass, West Anstruther | 25 Sept. 1580 | Steven Arnot | 12 | ? |
| George Christie, Dysart | 7 Sept. 1569 | George Corstorphine | 12 | 13-0-0 |
| do. | 7 Sept. 1569 | William Davidson | 24 | ? |
| do. | 7 Sept. 1569 | James Dingwall | 12 | 13-0-0 |
| Andrew Clark | 28 Sept. 1590 | George Gilruth | 6 | 22-0-0 |
| Thomas Clark | 16 Sept. 1571 | Arthur Gray | 12 | 26-0-0 |
| do. | 22 Sept. 1571 | William Gilbert | 6 | 14-10-0 |
| Robert Constable, Wellington | 19 Oct. 1569 | John Bowsie, William Kay | 18 | 54-0-0 |
| do. | 20 Oct. 1569 | do. do. | 24 | 72-0-0 |
| Margaret Cornwall, Patrick Geddes's widow | 17 May 1576 | John Arrock | 12 | ? |
| do. | 7 Sept. 1576 | Arthur Gray | 18 | 46-0-0 |
| do. | 9 Sept. 1577 | do. | 18 | ? |
| George Corstorphine | 29 Apr. 1583 | Steven Arnot, Crail, George Bell, Fisherrow | 1,000 fresh ling | ? |

| Merchant | Date | Contractor | Barrels | £Scots |
|---|---|---|---|---|
| William Corstorphine elder | 11 Sept. 1576 | John Lumsden | 6 | 23-0-0 |
| do. | 12 Sept.1576 | George Peirson | 12 | ? |
| do. | 15 Sept. 1576 | George Corstorphine | 12 | 16-0-0 |
| Alan Cunningham | 3 Sept. 1582 | Arthur Gray | 12 | ? |
| do. | 3 Sept. 1582 | John Davidson | 6 | ? |
| do. | 19 Sept. 1582 | John Melville | 24 | ? |
| do. | 20 Sept. 1582 | Thomas Beane, Thomas Blair | 36 | ? |
| do. | 21 Sept. 1582 | John Bruce | 6 | ? |
| do. | 21 Sept. 1582 | Alexander Simson | 12 | ? |
| do. | 27 Aug. 1583 | John Davidson | 24 | 62-0-0 |
| do. | 10 Sept. 1583 | John Ellis | 12 | 32-0-0 |
| do. | 18 Sept. 1583 | John Greif | 14 | 14-0-0 |
| do. | 18 Sept. 1583 | Alexander Simson | 20 | 20-0-0 |
| do. | 19 Sept. 1583 | Thomas Beane | 24 | 34-0-0 |
| do. | 19 Sept. 1583 | Edward Spens | 6 | 8-10-0 |
| William Currour/ Symon Spens | 25 Aug. 1590 | William Hunter | 66 | ? |
| John Davidson, baxter | 21 Sept. 1576 | John Dawson | 12 | ? |
| John Dingwall | 29 Sept. 1568 | Alexander Bikarton | 6 | 12-0-0 |
| do. | 29 Sept. 1568 | David Hawson | 7 | 14-0-0 |
| do. | 15 Sept. 1569 | William Burgess | 12 | ? |
| do. | 15 Sept. 1569 | John Gardiner | 36 | ? |
| do. | 26 Sept. 1569 | George Kid | 12 | ? |

| Merchant | Date | Contractor | Barrels | £Scots |
|---|---|---|---|---|
| do. | 29 Sept. 1569 | Alexander Bikarton (6), William Gilbert (12) | 18 | 26-0-0 |
| John Dougall, Crail | 8 Sept. 1583 | Thomas Blair (24) John Martin (12) | 36 | 35-0-0 |
| John Dougall younger, Edinburgh | 11 Sept. 1581 | John Reid | 18 | ? |
| do. | 12 Sept. 1581 | John Martin | 12 | ? |
| do. | 12 Sept. 1581 | George Peirson | 24 | ? |
| Patrick Dyk | 7 Sept. 1571 | Andro Baxter | 12 | 28-0-0 |
| Alexander Farmer | 20 Sept. 1573 | Thomas Morris | 6 | ? |
| do. | 25 Sept. 1580 | John Wilson | 6 | ? |
| Thomas Farmer | 19 Aug. 1582 | William Kay | 12 | ? |
| Robert Fyndlayson, Dundee | 6 Sept. 1583 | John Edyson | 6 | 10-0-0 |
| do. | 6 Sept. 1583 | Alexander Kinnaird | 12 | 20-0-0 |
| John Fyschars | 8 Sept. 1583 | William Lyall | 12 | 36-0-0 |
| James Geddy | 8 Sept. 1583 | William Lyall | 48 | ? |
| do. | 17 Sept. 1583 | Robert Dingwall | 12 | ? |
| Margaret Gowan | 16 Sept. 1579 | William Arnot | 12 | 20-0-0 |
| David Grig, St Andrews | 13 Sept. 1590 | Androw Davidson | 13 | ? |
| Edward Grig | 23 Sept. 1571 | Andro Wilson | 6 | 13-0-0 |
| do. | 22 Nov. 1581 | Arthur Gray | 6 | ? |
| do. | 27 Aug. 1582 | Androw Daw | 6 | ? |
| do. | 21 Sept. 1582 | Robert Dingwall | 6 | ? |
| John Holbetar | 28 Aug. 1576 | Alexander Wemyss | 12 | ? |

| Merchant | Date | Contractor | Barrels | £Scots |
|---|---|---|---|---|
| Thomas Hall, Prestonpans | 12 Sept. 1570 | Andro Corstorphine Andro Peirson | 24 | 28-0-0 |
| John Hamilton, Edinburgh | 2 May 1583 | Steven Arnot George Bell | 1,500 keiling | ? |
| Ninian Hamilton | 2 Sept. 1574 | John Greif | 6 | 23-0-0 |
| do. | 27 Aug. 1576 | Thomas Beane | 18 | ? |
| do. | 7 Sept. 1576 | John Greif | 6 | 6-0-0 |
| do. | 29 Sept. 1576 | John Caddowy, Anstruther | 12 | 30-0-0 |
| do. | 26 May 1579 | Robert Ballie | 12 | 22-0-0 |
| John Harte, Canongate | 26 Aug. 1576 | Thomas Martin | 12 | ? |
| do. | 26 Aug. 1576 | Andro Bikarton, James Martin | 12+12 | ? |
| do. | 4 Sept. 1576 | James Martin Alexander Woede | 12+12 | ? |
| do. | 7 Sept. 1576 | Peter and Robert Arnot | 24 | 60-0-0 |
| do. | 7 Sept. 1576 | Steven Arnot | 24 | 60-0-0 |
| do. | 7 Sept. 1576 | William Arnot | 24 | 60-0-0 |
| do. | 7 Sept. 1576 | George Corstorphine | 12 | 30-0-0 |
| do. | 9 Sept. 1576 | Robert Dawson | 12 | ? |
| do. | 12 Sept. 1576 | Alexander Reid | 6 | ? |
| do. | 29 Apr. 1578 | Robert Arnot | 12 | ? |
| do. | 19 Sept. 1578 | Robert Arnot, John Bowsie | 12 | ? |
| do. | 14 Sept. 1580 | Thomas Kinninmonth | 12 | ? |

| Merchant | Date | Contractor | Barrels | £Scots |
|---|---|---|---|---|
| do. | 16 Sept. 1580 | Thomas Mayerton | 18 | ? |
| do. | 18 Sept. 1580 | Robert Arnot | 12 | ? |
| do. | 25 Sept.1580 | John Corstorphine John Mayerton | 6 | ? |
| do. | 25 Sept.1580 | Patrick Dyk | 6 | ? |
| do. | 25 Sept.1580 | Alexander Farmer | 18 | ? |
| do. | 30 Aug. 1581 | Arthur Gray | 12 | ? |
| do. | 30 Aug. 1581 | Arthur Gray William Kay | 12+12 | ? |
| do. | 19 Nov. 1581 | Arthur Gray, John Paterson | 24 | 60-0-0 |
| do. | 24 Sept.1582 | William Robertson | 12 | 22-0-0 |
| William Hawson | 5 Sept. 1577 | John Burgess, Thomas Kinninmonth, Thomas Morris | 10 | ? |
| Patrick Hogg, Kirkcaldy | 7 Sept. 1576 | George Peirson | 24 | 64-0-0 |
| do. | 7 Sept. 1576 | James Cass, James Dingwall, John Martin | 36 | 32-0-0 |
| do. | 7 Sept. 1576 | John Dawson | 36 | 96-0-0 |
| do. | 4 Oct. 1577 | John Dawson | 36 | 135-0-0 |
| do. | 6 May 1580 | Robert Dingwall | 12 | ? |
| do. | 6 May 1580 | Arthur Gray | 6 | ? |
| William Hunter | 19 Nov. 1579 | Arthur Gray | 16 | ? |
| Archibald Kay | 18 Apr. 1581 | Robert Dingwall | 2 | 6-0-0 |

| Merchant | Date | Contractor | Barrels | £Scots |
|---|---|---|---|---|
| Thomas Kay | 16 Sept. 1571 | Robert Arnot | 12 | 28-0-0 |
| do. | 16 Sept. 1571 | Andro Baxter | 6 | 14-0-0 |
| do. | 23 Sept. 1571 | Andro Wilson | 3 | 6-10-0 |
| William Kay | 13 Oct. 1555 | Robert & William Gray | 15,000 herring | ? |
| Andro Lindsay | 16 Sept. 1577 | Arthur Gray | 6 | 23-6-8 |
| do. | 6 May 1578 | William Arnot | 6 | ? |
| Henry Lindsay | 20 Sept. 1577 | William Arnot | 24 | 40-0-0 |
| John Lindsay, Cupar | 30 Aug. 1577 | John Spens | 12 | ? |
| Patrick Lindsay | 23 Sept. 1570 | Andro Corstorphine Andro Peirson | 10 | 25-0-0 |
| do. | 27 Sept. 1570 | Alexander Bikarton | 12 | ? |
| do. | 27 Sept. 1570 | John Corstorphine | 12 | ? |
| do. | 28 Sept. 1570 | Thomas Morrison | 1 | 1-0-0 |
| do. | 6 Oct. 1570 | Alexander Woede | 5 | 12-5-0 |
| do. | 11 Sept. 1571 | John Arnot | 12 | 26-0-0 |
| do. | 11 Sept. 1571 | John & Peter Arnot | 18 | 39-0-0 |
| do. | 13 Sept. 1571 | Alexander Woede | 6 | 13-0-0 |
| do. | 23 Sept. 1571 | William Burgess | 1 | 3-0-0 |
| do. | 18 Sept. 1572 | Andro Baxter | 12 | 26-0-0 |
| do. | 24 Sept. 1572 | Andro Bikarton | 36 ? (a) | 72-0-0 |
| do. | 26 Sept. 1572 | Andro Baxter | 1 | ? |
| do. | 4 Sept. 1573 | Robert Arrock | 12 | 35-0-0 |
| do. | 6 Sept. 1573 | Andro Baxter | 12 | 12-0-0 |

| Merchant | Date | Contractor | Barrels | £Scots |
|---|---|---|---|---|
| do. | 10 Sept. 1573 | do. | 6 | 4-0-0 |
| do. | 18 Sept. 1573 | do. | 7 | ? |
| do. | 31 May 1576 | John Smith | 12 | ? |
| do. | 9 Sept. 1576 | Andro Bikarton | 6 | ? |
| do. | 13 Sept. 1576 | Thomas Simson | 12 | ? |
| do. | 16 Sept. 1576 | Robert Arnot | 12 | ? |
| do. | 18 Apr. 1577 | Robert Arnot | 12 | ? |
| do. | 20 Apr. 1577 | Arthur Gray | 12 | ? |
| do. | 6 Sept. 1577 | John Bruce, Arthur Gray | 6 | ? |
| do. | 8 Sept. 1577 | William Currour | 9 | 8-0-0 |
| do. | 17 Sept. 1577 | Thomas Simson | 12 | ? |
| do. | 21 Sept. 1577 | Robert & Steven Arnot | 12 | ? |
| do. | 30 Nov. 1577 | Arthur Gray | 12 | 42-0-0 |
| do. | 30 Sept. 1578 | James Cass | 21 | ? |
| Patrick Littlejohn, St Andrews | 10 Sept. 1580 | Robert Dingwall | 6 | ? |
| David Logemonth | 3 Sept. 1577 | Andro Stevenson | 12 | ? |
| John Lumsden | 23 Sept. 1567 | George Davidson | 12 | 28-0-0 |
| William Lyall | 21 Sept. 1580 | Robert Dingwall | 6 | ? |
| John MacMoran, Edinburgh | 7 Sept. 1582 | John Browne, Arthur Gray | 18 | 51-0-0 |
| do. | 7 Sept. 1582 | John Smyt | 24 | 68-0-0 |
| George Martin, Mayerton | 7 Sept. 1581 | Robert Alexander | 12 | ? |
| do. | 13 Sept. 1581 | John Wilson | 12 | ? |
| do. | 8 Sept. 1582 | John Wilson | 12 | 32-0-0 |
| Thomas Martin | 3 Sept. 1576 | Robert Dawson | 18 | 45-0-0 |

| Merchant | Date | Contractor | Barrels | £Scots |
|---|---|---|---|---|
| George Meldrum | 15 Sept. 1569 | William Young | 24 | 49-0-0 |
| do. | 27 Sept. 1569 | Andro Corstorphine | 6 | 12-0-0 |
| do. | 14 Oct. 1569 | Thomas Martin | 12 | 24-0-0 |
| do. | 24 Nov. 1579 | Thomas Davidson younger | 18 | ? |
| James Meldrum | 12 Sept. 1576 | George Peirson | 24 | ? |
| do. | 14 Sept. 1576 | William Hawson | 18 | ? |
| do. | 18 Sept. 1576 | David Scott | 24 | 60-0-0 |
| Andrew Melville younger | 17 Sept. 1579, cf 23 Febr. 1579/80 | John Melville younger | 12 | ? |
| John Melville, Melvyne elder | 2 September 1573 | William Annand, Alexander Farmer | 24 (WA 18, AF 6) | 58-0-0 |
| do. | 27 May 1578 | Andro Melville, Anstruther | 14 | 43-3-4 |
| do. younger | 18 Sept. 1581 | Robert Alexander, John Bruce | 21 (RA 9, JB 12) | ? |
| do. | 21 Apr. 1582 | John Bruce | 6 | ? |
| do. | 21 Apr. 1582 | John Davidson | 6 | ? |
| do. | 9 May 1582 | Thomas Beane, William Bowsie | 12 | ? |
| do. | 1 June 1582 | Thomas Patie, younger | 6 | ? |
| do. | 12 Sept. 1582 | John Paterson | 12 | ? |
| do. | 15 Sept. 1590 | Alexander Farmer | 6 | ? |
| do. | 28 Sept. 1590 | Androw Davidson | 9 | 30-0-0 |

| Merchant | Date | Contractor | Barrels | £Scots |
|---|---|---|---|---|
| William Melville | 12 Sept. 1576 | Arthur Gray | 12 | 32-0-0 |
| do. | 14 Sept. 1576 | Robert Dingwall | 12 | 32-0-0 |
| do. | 16 Sept. 1576 | William Annand | 36 | 96-0-0 |
| do. | 19 Sept. 1576 | Alexander Farmer | 36 | 96-0-0 |
| James Monipenny | 1 Sept. 1571 | George Corstorphine | 9 | 20-0-0 |
| William Monipenny | 12 Sept. 1589 | William Daw | 48 | 176-0-0 |
| George Morton | 14 Sept. 1583 | John Wilson | 18 | 46-0-0 |
| William Morton, cooper | 14 Sept. 1576 | James Corstorphine | 6 | 15-10-0 |
| do. | 1 Sept. 1577 | Robert Ottar | 12 | 31-0-0 |
| do. | 3 Sept. 1577 | James Corstorphine | 12 | ? |
| do. | 9 Sept. 1577 | Alexander Woed | 18 | ? |
| do. | 17 Sept. 1577 | John Ottar | 12 | ? |
| do. | 24 Sept. 1577 | William Daw | 6 | ? |
| do. | 12 Apr. 1580 | William Smyth, cooper | 2 | ? |
| do. | 12 May 1580 | Robert Morris | 1 | ? |
| do. | 30 Aug. 1580 | John Balcony | 12 | ? |
| do. | 14 Sept. 1580 | Thomas Blair | 24 | ? |
| do. | 14 Sept. 1580 | Alexander Kynnaird | 12 | ? |
| do. | 15 Sept. 1580 | Thomas Blair, John Corstorphine younger | 12 | ? |
| do. | 21 Mar. 1580/1 | Arthur Gray | 12 | ? |
| do. | 3 Sept. 1581 | William Smyth | 1 | ? |
| do. | 13 Sept. 1581 | John Martin | 12 | ? |

| Merchant | Date | Contractor | Barrels | £Scots |
|---|---|---|---|---|
| do. | 14 Sept. 1581 | Robert Alexander, John Bruce, Alexander Kinnaird | 17 (RA 3, JB 2, AK 12) | ? |
| do. | 30 Dec.1581 | Alexander Kinnaird | 12 | ? |
| do. | 27 Febr. 1581/2 | John Balcony | 12 | ? |
| do. | 26 Mar. 1582 | Androw & John Annand | 7 | ? |
| do. | 26 Mar. 1582 | Arthur Gray | 12 | ? |
| do. | 1 June 1582 | Edward Abay, John Wilson | 18 (EA 12, JW 6) | ? |
| do. | 3 Sept. 1582 | John Balcony | 18 | ? |
| Thomas Myrton | 1 Sept. 1590 | Androw Davidson | 9 | 30-0-0 |
| William Napier, Edinburgh | Before 30 Nov. 1583 | Robert Arnot | 25 | ? |
| James Nicoll, Edinburgh | 17 June 1572 | John Davidson | 168 | ? |
| Christine Oliphant | 7 Oct. 1582 | Andro Annand | 24 | ? |
| do. | 7 Oct. 1582 | John Smyt | 24 | ? |
| David Page, Cupar | 26 Aug. 1577 | William Currour, Robert King, Thomas Simson | 12+12 +12 | ? |
| William Powsta, Cellardyke | 12 May 1574 | William Culiwork (?) | 1 dozen dry fish | ? |
| do. | 13 Sept. 1590 | Thomas Dawson | 100 herring + 4 salt fish keiling | 45-0-0 |

| Merchant | Date | Contractor | Barrels | £Scots |
|---|---|---|---|---|
| John Ramsay | 20 Sept. 1569 | William "Obondis" | 2 | 4-6-8 |
| Alexander Reid, Prestonpans | 3 Sept. 1569 | George Davidson | 12 | 26-0-0 |
| do. | 21 Aug. 1570 | Patrick Geddes | 6 | ? |
| do. | 12 Sept. 1570 | William Kay, Thomas Martin | 42 | 96-5-0 |
| do. | 8 Sept. 1571 | John Bowsie | 21 | 49-0-0 |
| do. | 10 Sept. 1571 | John Reid | 24 | 56-0-0 |
| do. | 10 Sept. 1571 | Alexander Farmer | 12 | 17-0-0 |
| do. | 10 Sept. 1571 | Thomas Martin | 12 | 28-0-0 |
| John Reid | 16 Sept. 1571 | William Hawson | 6 | ? |
| John Simson | 6 Sept. 1580 | Robert Arnot | 18 | ? |
| do. | 6 Sept. 1580 | John Calvert | 24 | ? |
| do. | 8 Sept. 1580 | John Balcony | 18 | ? |
| do. | 6 Sept. 1581 | Robert Arnot | 12 | ? |
| John Simson younger | 15 Sept. 1580 | William Lyall | 24 | ? |
| do. | 10 Sept. 1582 | William Bowsie | 20 | 34-0-0 |
| John Spens | 25 Sept. 1572 | Steven Arnot | 12 | ? |
| William Spens | 23 Sept. 1576 | John Dawson | 6 | ? |
| do. | 7 Febr. 1583/4 | Edward Spens | 14 | ? |
| William Stirling, Edinburgh | 25 Sept. 1570 | John Dawson | 30 | 67-10-0 |
| James Summerville, Edinburgh | 3 Sept. 1580 | Robert King younger | 8 | ? |
| do. | 2 Sept. 1581 | Arthur Gray | 24 | ? |
| do. | 7 Febr. 1582/3 | Thomas Robertson | 6 keiling | ? |
| John Summerville, Edinburgh | 17 Nov. 1581 | Arthur Gray | 24 | 60-0-0 |

| Merchant | Date | Contractor | Barrels | £Scots |
|---|---|---|---|---|
| do. | 30 Mar. 1584 | John Martin, Edward Spens | 12 | ? |
| James Sydserf, Edinburgh | 1 Sept. 1590 | Androw Davidson | 12 | 60-0-0 |
| do. | 18 Sept. 1590 | Alexander Farmer | 18 | 66-0-0 |
| do. | 22 Sept. 1590 | Edward Abbey | 24 | 88-0-0 |
| do. | 22 Sept. 1590 | John Simson | 6 | 22-0-0 |
| do. | 22 Sept. 1590 | Androw Lonye | 6 | 22-10-0 |
| do. | 22 Sept. 1590 | John Gilruth | 6 | 22-10-0 |
| do. | 22 Sept. 1590 | John Alexander, Thomas Duncan, Alexander Farmer, John Galloway younger, John Simson | 12 | 44-0-0 |
| James Sydserf, Edinburgh | 22 Sept. 1590 | James Corstorphine elder | 9 | 33-15-0 |
| do. | 22 Sept. 1590 | JohnWitkow | 12 | 45-0-0 |
| Archibald Thomson, East Anstruther | 30 Sept.1580 | Steven Arnot | 18 | ? |
| John Traille, Dundee | 2 Sept. 1581 | William Lyall, Harry White | 36 (WL 24, HW 12) | ? |
| do. | 2 Sept. 1581 | Patrick Dyk | 12 | ? |
| Nicol Uddart, Edinburgh | 9 Sept. 1574 | William Davidson | 18 | 48-0-0 |
| do. | 10 Sept. 1574 | John Kay | 7 | 18-13-4 |
| do. | 10 Sept. 1574 | Thomas Morris | 6 | 16-0-0 |
| do. | 21 Sept. 1574 | William Kay | 12 | 32-0-0 |
| Charles Watson | 23 Sept. 1566 | Robert Muyr | 2 | ? |

| Merchant | Date | Contractor | Barrels | £Scots |
|---|---|---|---|---|
| John Welwood, St Andrews | 30 Aug. 1580 | John Gray | 12 | ? |
| do. | 17 Sept. 1583 | William Dawson | 6 | ? |
| Thomas Welwood, St Andrews | 23 Sept. 1570 | William Arnot | 6 | ? |
| do. | 12 June 1581 | John Paterson | 12 | ? |
| John Wemyss, Edinburgh | 16 Sept. 1570 | William Kay | 12 | 28-0-0 |
| do. | 16 Sept. 1570 | John Melville | 12 | 28-0-0 |
| James Williamson | 12 July 1590 | William Martin, Robert Morris, John Parkie | ? | 220-0-0 |
| Archibald Wishart St Andrews | 20 Sept. 1579 | Robert Dingwall | 12 | ? |
| do. | 26 Sept. 1581 | Steven Arnot, Robert Dingwall, | 18 | ? |
| do. | 12 Sept. 1582 | William Bowsie, Andro Fuirde | 6 | ? |
| do. | 12 Sept. 1582 | Steven Arnot | ? | ? |
| James Woede, son of Andro W., Largo | 18 Sept. 1577 | Thomas Abbey | 54 | ? |
| do. | 3 Dec. 1583 | Arthur Gray | 18 | 33-15-0 |
| James Woede, brother of Andro W., Largo | 29 Mar. 1580 | William Hawson | 12 | ? |
| James Woede, brother of Andro W., Largo | 18 Apr. 1581 | Arthur Gray | 12 | ? |
| do. | 25 Sept. 1581 | Robert Dingwall | 12 | ? |
| do. | 25 Sept. 1581 | John Smith | 18 | ? |
| Ninian Woede | 18 Sept. 1577 | Robert Ottar | 12 | ? |

| Merchant | Date | Contractor | Barrels | £Scots |
|---|---|---|---|---|
| do. | 21 Sept. 1577 | Alexander Farmer | 18 | ? |
| do. | 27 May 1579 | Robert Arnot | 18 | ? |
| do. | 4 Oct. 1580 | Alexander Farmer | 12 | ? |
| do. | 29 Mar. 1581 | John Reid | 24 | ? |
| do. | 26 Aug. 1581 | James Brownie, West Anstruther | 6 | ? |
| do. | 13 Sept. 1581 | Alexander Farmer | 42 | ? |
| do. | 14 Sept. 1581 | John Wilson | 18 | ? |
| do. | 3 Apr. 1582 | Thomas Beane | 6 | ? |
| do. | 11 Apr. 1582 | Edward Abbey | 18 | ? |
| do. | 13 Sept. 1582 | Arthur Gray | 78 | ? |
| do. | 20 Sept. 1590 | George Peirson | 12 | 44-0-0 |
| do. | 20 Sept. 1590 | Androw Davidson | 12 | 44-0-0 |
| do. | 22 Sept. 1590 | Alexander Farmer | 6 1/2 | 23-16-8 |
| James Woid, Pittenweem | 26 Sept. 1581 | John Alexander, Cellardyke | 12 | ? |
| Janet Young, William Lumsden's widow | 7 Sept. 1590 | Walter Annell | 6 | 22-0-0 |
| do. | 15 Sept. 1590 | John Selkirk | 6 | 22-0-0 |
| do. | 28 Sept. 1590 | John Martin | 6 | 22-10-0 |

a) Ms. 3, but the amount is excessive, if barrels and not lasts are meant.

*Source: ULStA B 10/8/1-8 Burgh Court Books of Crail 1552-95 various years.*

Table 22.  Activities by certain contractors

| Contractor | Year | Customs Accounts | Obligations (Barrels of Herring) |
|---|---|---|---|
| Thomas Abbey | 1570-1 | 132 barrels herring | - |
| | 1577 | - | 54 |
| Walter Annell | 1582-3 | 48 barrels herring | - |
| | 1590 | - | 6 |
| John Arnot | 1571 | 6,000 fish + English goods | 30 |
| | 1574 | 7,000 pale fish + English goods (twice) | - |
| | 1574-5 | 156 barrels Firth of Forth herring | - |
| | 1576-7 (a) | 168 barrels of (Loch Broom ?) herring + 6,000 pale fish | - |
| Robert Arnot | 1571 | 2,500 fish | 12 barrels |
| | 1574 | English goods | - |
| | 1576 | Firth of Forth herring | 30 |
| | 1577 | 60 barrels | 24 |
| | 1578 | - | 24 |
| | 1579 | - | 30 |
| | 1580 | - | 30 |
| | 1581 | - | 24 |
| | 1582/3 | - | 25 |
| William Arnot | 1566 | 50 barrels herring | - |
| | 1569 | - | 12 |
| | 1570/1 | 228 barrels herring + craytis (=crayfish) | 6 |
| | 1574 | English goods | - |

| Contractor | Year | Customs Accounts | Obligations (Barrels of Herring) |
|---|---|---|---|
| | 1574/5 | 156 barrels keiling | - |
| | 1576 | Firth of Forth herring | 24 |
| | 1577 | 144 barrels | 36 |
| | 1578 | - | 6 |
| | 1579 | - | 20 |
| John Balcony | 1570/1 | 1,600 fish | - |
| | 1580 | - | 30 |
| | 1582 | - | 30 |
| Andro Bikarton | 1569 | 800 fish | 44 |
| | 1570 | English goods | 12 |
| | 1572 | - | 36 |
| | 1573-5 | Norway goods | - |
| | 1574 | - | 12 |
| | 1576 | - | 36 |
| John Bowsie | 1569 | - | 42 |
| | 1573-5 | English goods | - |
| | 1574 | 1,200 fish + 120 barrels herring | - |
| William Bowsie | 1574/5 | Firth of Forth herring 120 barrels | - |
| | 1582 | - | 26 |
| John Brown(ie) | 1574 | English goods (twice), 2,500 pale fish | - |
| | 1574/5 | 4,400 pale fish | - |
| | 1582 | - | 18 |
| Andro Davidson elder | 1570/1 | 2,200 fish | - |
| | 1577 | - | 18 |

| Contractor | Year | Customs Accounts | Obligations (Barrels of Herring) |
|---|---|---|---|
| | 1590 | - | 12 |
| Thomas Davidson younger | 1579 | - | 18 |
| Andro Daw, Largo | 1570/1 | 144 barrels of herring | - |
| | 1582 | - | 6 |
| Robert Dingwall | 1576 | - | 12 |
| | 1576/7 | Firth of Forth herring 120 barrels | - |
| | 1579 | - | 12 |
| | 1580 | - | 24 |
| | 1581 | - | 14 |
| | 1582 | - | 6 |
| | 1583 | - | 12 |
| Alexander Farmer | 1569 | - | 12 |
| | 1571 | - | 20 |
| | 1573 | - | 24 |
| | 1574/5 | Firth of Forth herring 120 barrels | - |
| | 1576 | - | 36 |
| | 1577 | - | 18 |
| | 1580 | - | 30 |
| | 1581 | - | 42 |
| | 1590 | - | 30 1/2 |
| Patrick Geddes | 1570 | - | 6 |
| | 1570/1 | 3,200 fish + salt | - |
| John Gray | 1570/1 | 2,600 fish | - |
| | 1580 | - | 12 |

| Contractor | Year | Customs Accounts | Obligations (Barrels of Herring) |
|---|---|---|---|
| William Hunter | 1576/7 | Firth of Forth herring 120 barrels | - |
| | 1590 | - | 66 |
| John Kay | 1566 | 156 barrels herring (b) | - |
| | 1574 | - | 7 |
| | 1574/5 | Norway goods | - |
| JohnLumsden | 1574/5 | 2,500 pale fish | - |
| | 1576 | Firth of Forth herring 144 barrels | - |
| | 1579 | - | 6 |
| John Melville/ Melvyne elder | 1570 | - | 12 |
| John Melville younger | 1579 | - | 12 |
| | 1582 | - | 54 (in two instalments) |
| George Peirson | 1570/1 | 2,000 fish | - |
| | 1574/5 | 36 barrels herring, English goods | - |
| | 1576 | 24 barrels (Loch Broom ?) herring + Norway stuling = 12 barrels salt + 2 dozen cloth | 60 |
| | 1581 | - | 24 |
| | 1590 | - | 12 |
| Alexander Simson | 1570/1 | 1,600 fish | - |
| | 1582 | - | 12 |
| | 1583 | - | 20 |

| Contractor | Year | Customs Accounts | Obligations (Barrels of Herring) |
|---|---|---|---|
| John Simson | 1574 | 16,000 pale fish, English goods | - |
| | 1574/6 | 2,000 pale herring, Firth of Forth herring 84 barrels | - |
| | 1576/7 | Firth of Forth herring 108 barrels | - |
| | 1590 | - | 6 |
| John Smith | 1571 | - | 12 |
| | 1574/5 | 4,500 pale fish | - |
| | 1576 | - | 12 |
| | 1576/7 | Norway stuling = 12 barrels salt + 4 barrels malt | - |
| | 1581 | - | 18 |
| | 1582 | - | 48 |
| John Wilson | 1566 | 54 barrels herring | - |
| | 1570/1 | 2,000 fish | - |
| | 1574 | Norway goods | - |
| | 1582 | - | 6 |

a) The herring with John Harte. b) With Thomas Wiggan.

*Source: NAS. E 71/6/1-10: Customs Books Crail, Anstruther, Pittenweem 1557-1582, various years; Table 21.*

Table 23.  Goods declared at Dundee by inhabitants of Crail

| 1566-7 | Walter Hay | 6 barrels herring |
|---|---|---|
| | Patrick Lindsay | 9 barrels herring + 12 lasts herring with Alexander Ramsay of Dundee |
| | JohnLumsden | 7 barrels herring |
| | George Meldrum | 2 ½ lasts herring |
| | Andro Robertson (?) | 6 lasts herring |
| 1574-5 (a) | James Annell | 11 lasts Loch Broom/Loch Carron herring |
| | William Annell | 4 lasts herring |
| | Robert Davidson | 18 lasts Loch Broom/Loch Carron herring |
| 1577-1578/9 | William Annand | 6 barrels herring |
| 1578/9-1579/80 | William Hunter | 600 schoirlingis (b), 600 lambskins, 200 goatskins |
| | Patrick Lindsay | 50 skins, 50 schoirlingis (b) |
| 1582 | William Hunter | 11 dozen cloth |

a) In this customs book the inhabitants of Anstruther and Crail form one group. Only the certain cases for Crail have been considered. b) Schoirling, ie the skin of a recently shorn sheep.

*Source: NAS. E 71/12/7-11.*

Table 24.  Goods declared at Edinburgh/Leith by inhabitants of Crail

| 15 Febr. 1573/4 -1 Nov. 1574 | Andro Melville, Anstruther | 130 skins |
|---|---|---|
| | John Wilson | 5 dozen cloth, 100 keiling |
| 1 Oct. 1575 -1 Oct. 1576 | Andro Davidson | 7 barrels salt |
| | William Lyall | 16 dozen cloth, 200 white leather, 14 daker hides |

|  | John Wilson | 15 dozen cloth, 200 skins, 6 daker hides |
| 1 Oct. 1578 -1 Oct. 1579 | William Currour | 14 chalders salt |
|  | John Wilson | 400 white leather |
| 1 Oct. 1579 -1 Oct. 1580 | William Lyall | 2 dozen cloth |
|  | John Wilson | 400 skins, 2 daker hides, 40 s. "Waly/ Wax" money (a) |
| 10 Sept. 1580 -1 Aug. 1581 | William Annand (b) | 4 lasts herring |
| 1 Oct. 1589 -1 Oct. 1590 | John Kay | 91 dozen cloth, 90 skins, 2 daker hides, 9 barrels ash and soap, paid 5s. for harthorns and 6s. for "Ginger" (?) money |
|  | Thomas Kay | 2 dozen cloth |
|  | Patrick Lindsay | Paid £3-8-0 for English goods |
|  | William Spens | 24 dozen cloth |
|  | John Wilson elder | 100 skins |
|  | John Wilson | 27 dozen cloth, 540 skins, 540 futefells (c), 42 daker hides, 21 daker hides with William Rig, 7 barrels butter/oil, paid 15s. wax money and £8-10-10 for English goods |
| 1 Oct. 1589 -1 Oct. 1590 | Andro Bikarton (b) | 4 lasts 6 barrels herring |

a) Can be read as Waly or as Wax, as the latter reading gives sense, I have preferred it.
b) Town of residence wrongly given as Anstruther. c) Skin of a lamb which has died soon after being dropped.

*Source: NAS. E 71/30/18-22 and E 71/32/9-10.*

Table 25.  Fishing activities by certain merchants

| Merchant | Year | Customs accounts | Obligations (Barrels of Herring) |
|---|---|---|---|
| William Annand | 1569 | - | 93 |
| | 1570 | - | 15 |
| | 1571 | - | 20 |
| | 1576 | 72 barrels keiling | 24 |
| | 1581 | - | 6 |
| | 1582 | - | 6 |
| Walter Ballingall | 1574 | - | 12 |
| | 1576 | - | 78 |
| | 1577 | - | 36 |
| | 1580 | - | 12 |
| David Beane | 1570-1 | 2,200 fishes | - |
| | 1571 | - | 38 |
| | 1572 | - | 30 |
| | 1574 | - | 18 |
| | 1574-5 | 108 barrels of Forth herring + English goods | - |
| William Beane | 1570-1 | 66 barrels of herring + 2,500 fishes | - |
| | 1571 | - | 12 |
| | 1573 | - | 18 |
| | 1574 | Norway goods | - |
| Thomas Blair | 1569 | - | 1 |
| | 1580 | - | 24 |
| George Christie, Dysart | 1569 | - | 48 |
| Thomas Clark | 1571 | - | 18 |

| Merchant | Year | Customs accounts | Obligations (Barrels of Herring) |
|---|---|---|---|
| Robert Constable, Wellington, England | 1569 | - | 42 |
| Margaret Cornwall Patrick Geddes | 1576 | - | 30 |
| | 1577 | - | 18 |
| William Corstorphine elder | 1576 | - | 30 |
| Alan Cunningham | 1573-5 | Salt | - |
| | 1574-5 | Train-oil | - |
| | 1582 | - | 96 |
| | 1583 | - | 100 |
| John Dingwall ~ Helen Bethell | 1566 | 264 barrels herring | - |
| | 1568 | - | 13 |
| | 1569 | - | 78 |
| | 1571 | - | 12 |
| Robert Dingwall | 1576-7 | 120 barrels Forth herring | - |
| John Dougall younger, Edinburgh | 1581 | - | 54 |
| | 1582 | Train-oil | - |
| Alexander Farmer | 1573 | - | 6 |
| | 1580 | - | 6 |
| Robert Findlayson, Dundee | 1583 | - | 18 |
| | 1584 | 1 tun of Bordeaux wine | - |
| | 1588 | Danzig goods (1 shippund lynt + five lasts of "lit" = dye) | - |
| James Geddy | 1583 | - | 60 |
| Edward Grig | 1571 | - | 6 |

| Merchant | Year | Customs accounts | Obligations (Barrels of Herring) |
|---|---|---|---|
| | 1581 | - | 6 |
| | 1582 | - | 12 |
| Ninian Hamilton | 1574 | - | 6 |
| | 1576 | - | 36 |
| | 1579 | - | 12 |
| | 1590 | - | 1 |
| John Harte, Canongate | 1576 | - | 162 |
| | 1576-7 | 168 barrels of herring with John Arnot | - |
| | 1578 | - | 24 |
| | 1580 | - | 72 |
| | 1581 | - | 60 |
| | 1582 | - | 12 |
| Patrick Hogg, Kirkcaldy | 1576 | - | 96 |
| | 1577 | - | 36 |
| | 1580 | - | 18 |
| William Hunter | 1576-7 | 120 barrels Forth herring | - |
| | 1579 | - | 16 |
| | 1581 | - | 3 1/2 |
| | 1582-3 | 4,000 pale fish (a) | - |
| | 1590 | - | 66 |
| Thomas Kay | 1569 | - | 12 with Alexander Airth |
| | 1571 | - | 21 |
| | 1573-5 | 3,000 pale fish | - |
| | 1574 | 2,200 pale fish + train-oil + 108 barrels herring + English goods (twice) | - |

| Merchant | Year | Customs accounts | Obligations (Barrels of Herring) |
|---|---|---|---|
| | 1574-5 | 120 barrels Forth herring + (twice) English goods | - |
| | 1576-7 | 120 barrels herring + 120 barrels Forth herring + 24 barrels herring + 4,000 pale fish | - |
| Andro Lindsay, wright | 1577 | - | 6 |
| | 1578 | - | 6 |
| Henry/Harry Lindsay | 1577 | - | 24 |
| | 1578 | - | 2 |
| Patrick Lindsay | 1566 | 144 barrels herring with Alexander Ramsay | - |
| | 1570 | - | 39 |
| | 1571 | - | 37 |
| | 1572 | - | 49 |
| | 1573 | - | 38 |
| | 1576 | - | 42 |
| | 1577 | - | 75 |
| | 1578 | - | 21 |
| John Mac Morran, Edinburgh | 1582 | - | 42 |
| | 1582-3 | 72 barrels herring | - |
| George Martin, Mayerton | 1581 | - | 24 |
| | 1582 | - | 12 |
| | 1583 | - | 18 |
| George Meldrum | 1566 | 6 barrels herring (with Patrick Rege (?) and James Hircor (?)) + 48 barrels herring | - |
| | 1569 | - | 42 |

| Merchant | Year | Customs accounts | Obligations (Barrels of Herring) |
|---|---|---|---|
| | 1570-1 | 20 barrels barrelfish + hides | - |
| | 1579 | - | 18 |
| James Meldrum | 1576 | - | 66 |
| | 1576-7 | 120 barrels Forth herring (with David Ramsay) | - |
| Andro Melville, Anstruther | 1573-5 | English goods | - |
| | 1574-5 | 60 barrels Forth herring + 9,000 pale fish | - |
| | 1579 | - | 12 |
| John Melville, Melvyne elder | 1573 | - | 24 |
| | 1573-5 | 18 barrels (herring ?) | - |
| | 1574-5 | 210 barrels Forth herring + 228 barrels packed keiling | - |
| | 1576-7 | Norway stuling (b) 10 barrels salt + 2 dozen cloth | - |
| | 1578 | - | 14 |
| John Melville younger | 1581 | - | 21 |
| | 1582 | - | 42 |
| | 1590 | - | 15 |
| William Melville | 1576 | - | 96 |
| Christine Oliphant | 1581 | - | 1/2 |
| | 1582 | - | 48 |
| William Powsta, Cellardyke | 1574 | - | 1 dozen dry fish |
| | 1590 | - | 100 herring + 4 salt fish keiling |

| Merchant | Year | Customs accounts | Obligations (Barrels of Herring) |
|---|---|---|---|
| Alexander Reid, Prestonpans | 1569 | - | 12 |
| | 1570 | - | 48 |
| | 1570-1 | 60 barrels herring + 24 barrels barrelfish | - |
| | 1571 | - | 69 |
| John Simson elder | 1574 | 21,000 pale fish + English goods | - |
| | 1574-5 | 84 barrels Forth herring + 2,000 pale fish | - |
| | 1580 | - | 60 |
| | 1581 | - | 12 |
| John Simson younger | 1580 | - | 24 |
| | 1582 | - | 20 |
| William Spens | 1576 | - | 6 |
| | 1584 | - | 14 |
| James Summerville, Edinburgh | 1580 | - | 8 |
| | 1581 | - | 24 |
| | 1583 | - | 6 barrels keiling |
| John Summerville, Edinburgh | 1581 | - | 24 |
| | 1584 | - | 12 |
| James Sydserf, Edinburgh | 1590 | - | 105 |
| John Traille, Dundee | 1581 | - | 48 |
| | 1582 | 42 barrels keiling | - |
| Nicol Uddart, Edinburgh | 1574 | - | 43 |

| Merchant | Year | Customs accounts | Obligations (Barrels of Herring) |
|---|---|---|---|
| John Welwood, St Andrews | 1580 | - | 12 |
| | 1583 | - | 6 |
| Thomas Welwood, St Andrews | 1570 | - | 6 |
| | 1581 | - | 12 |
| | 1582-3 | 120 barrels keiling | - |
| John Wemyss, Edinburgh | 1570 | - | 24 |
| Archibald Wishart, St Andrews | 1579 | - | 12 |
| | 1581 | - | 18 |
| | 1582 | - | 6 |
| James Woede elder, brother of Andro W., Largo | 1570-1 | 72 barrels herring | - |
| | 1573-5 | 48 barrels herring (?) + 3 barrels salmon | - |
| | 1580 | - | 12 |
| | 1581 | - | 42 |
| James Woede younger, son of Andro W., Largo | 1577 | - | 54 |
| | 1583 | - | 18 |
| Ninian Woede | 1574-5 | 2,000 pale fish | - |
| | 1577 | 48 barrels herring + 2,500 pale fish | 30 |
| | 1579 | - | 18 |
| | 1581 | - | 90 |
| | 1582 | - | 102 |
| | 1590 | - | 30 1/2 |
| Janet Young | 1590 | - | 18 |

a) Fish of inferior size. b) Stuling, ie commodities used as ballast.

Source: NAS. E 71/6/1-10: Customs Books Pittenweem, Anstruther and Crail 1557-1582, various years; ULStA B 10/8/1-8 Burgh Court Books of Crail 1552-1595 various years.

Table 26.   Goods entered at Edinburgh/Leith by the two merchants John Dougall

| Account | Merchant | Goods declared |
|---|---|---|
| 15 Dec. 1573 -1 Nov. 1574 | John Dougall | 2 dozen cloth, 60 futefells, paid £5-10-0 customs for English goods |
| 1 Oct. 1575 -1 Oct. 1576 | John Dougall Son | 6 dozen cloth |
| | John Dougall | 11 dozen cloth, 100 skins, 9 daker hides, paid £1-6-8 customs for English goods |
| 1 Oct. 1578 -1 Oct.1579 | John Dougall | 56 dozen cloth (minimum), 30 skins, 36 daker hides, 6 barrels herring/codling, 6 tuns wine, 1 puncheon wine, paid £10-14-7 customs for English goods |
| 1 Oct. 1579 -1 Oct.1580 | John Dougall | 71 dozen cloth, 490 skins, 19 daker hides, 1 barrel salmon, 2 tuns wine, paid £15-0-0 customs for English goods |
| 1 Oct. 1589 -1 Oct. 1590 | John Dougall elder | 54 dozen cloth, 3 lasts (?), 19 daker hides |

*Source: NAS. E 71/30/18-22.*

# Glossary

| Older Expression | Modern Equivalent |
|---|---|
| Aiken ruiffe spairs | Oaken roof spars |
| Baringe | Freight |
| Blawn | Wind dried |
| Bow | Buoy |
| Bow towis | Buoy ropes |
| Broum loumis | Brewing lum |
| Cadoraun | Cauldron |
| Craytis | Crayfish |
| Daillis | Deals |
| Daker | A number of ten, especially hides |
| Elnis | Ells |
| Feand | Charter (eg of a ship) |
| Fiar | Calculated average price of corn |
| Firrikin | A firkin – i.e. small cask for liquids, butter, fish etc., as a measure 36.4-40.95 litres |
| Flimis byndtreis | Wood for making barrels Flemish bind |
| Foged | Representative of the Crown (Shetland) |
| Futefell | Skin of a lamb which has died soon after being dropped |
| Fyrue dailes | Fir deals |
| Girdis | Barrel hoops |
| Great, gryt salt | Foreign, mainly French or Spanish salt |
| Grethyng | Great line |

| | |
|---|---|
| Herring pryfe | Quality control of herring |
| Huikmaker | Anchorsmith |
| Keiling | Full size cod |
| Knappet = Knapholt | Clapboard |
| Knappis | Wooden vats |
| Laidstones | Leaden sinkers |
| Landkenning | Distance within land can be seen from the top of the mast |
| Lit | Dye |
| Lyuht mony | Light money (ie under the standard or legal weight) |
| Mwre | Moor |
| Owtreik, Outreik, Outreke | Equipping a ship with requisites for the voyage |
| Pale, palie, peill herring | Herring of inferior size |
| Satte | Coalfish, saithe |
| Satting | Storage ? |
| Schoirling | Skin of a recently shorn sheep |
| Skenis treeis | Wooden hafts for daggers (skeans) ? |
| Small salt | Scottish salt |
| Smallyng | Small line |
| Steyngis | Poles |
| Stuling | Commodities used as ballast |
| Stuiting | Props |
| Train-oil | Oil obtained from the blubber of a whale or other marine animal |

# Bibliography

## Unpublished sources

### Dundee City Archives

Lockit Book of Burgesses of Dundee 1513-1981.

Register of Ships 1580-1589.

### Edinburgh City Archives

SL 150/1/2: Burgh Court Book Canongate 1574-1577.

SL 150/1/3: Burgh Court Book Canongate 1577-1580.

SL 150/1/4: Burgh Court Book Canongate 1580-1583.

### National Archives of Scotland

NAS B 10/1/1, Protocol Book of Crail 1566/7-1574 and 1641-1652.

NAS B 10/1/2, Protocol Book of Crail 1589-1600.

NAS. E 71/6/1, Customs Book Pittenweem, Anstruther and Crail 1557

NAS. E 71/6/2, Customs Book Pittenweem, Anstruther and Crail 1566

NAS. E 71/6/3, Cocket Book Pittenweem, Anstruther and Crail 30 Sept. 1570-10 Oct. 1572

NAS. E 71/6/4, Customs Book Pittenweem, Anstruther and Crail 22 Oct.-27 Dec. 1573

NAS. E 71/6/5, Customs Book Pittenweem, Anstruther and Crail 26 Dec. 1573-6 Mar. 1574/5

NAS. E 71/6/6, Customs Book Pittenweem, Anstruther and Crail 31 Mar.-3 Nov. 1574

NAS. E 71/6/7, Duplicate of E 71/6/6

NAS. E 71/6/8, Customs Book Pittenweem, Anstruther and Crail 3 Nov. 1574-9 Nov. 1575

NAS. E 71/6/9, Cocket Book Pittenweem, Anstruther and Crail
14 Nov. 1576-18 Nov. 1577

NAS. E 71/6/10, Customs Book Pittenweem, Anstruther and Crail
21 Aug.-1 Oct. 1582

NAS. E 71/12/7, Entry Book of Cockets Dundee 1566-7

NAS. E 71/12/8, Entry Book of Cockets Dundee 13 Oct. 1574
-6 Nov. 1575

NAS. E 71/12/9, Customs Account Dundee 3 Dec. 1577-21 Jan.1578/9

NAS. E 71/12/10, Cocket Book Dundee 21 Jan. 1578/9-15 Jan. 1579/80

NAS. E 71/12/11, Customs Account Dundee 12 Aug.-1 Oct. 1582

NAS. E 71/30/18, Customs Account Edinburgh 15 Dec. 1573
-1 Nov. 1574

NAS. E 71/30/19, Customs Account Edinburgh 1 Oct. 1575-1 Oct. 1576

NAS. E 71/30/20, Customs Account Edinburgh 1 Oct. 1578-1 Oct.1579

NAS. E 71/30/21, Customs Account Edinburgh 1 Oct. 1579-1 Oct. 1580

NAS. E 71/30/22, Customs Account Edinburgh 1 Oct. 1589-1 Oct. 1590

NAS. E 71/32/9, Entry Book of Cockets Edinburgh 10 Sept. 1580
-1 Aug. 1581

NAS. E 71/32/10, Entry Book of Cockets Edinburgh 1 Oct.1589
-1 Oct. 1590

Rigsarkivet, Copenhagen

Øresundstoldregnskab 1562

Øresundstoldregnskab 1567

Øresundstoldregnskab 1569

Øresundstoldregnskab 1576 (Frederik Lyall)

Øresundstoldregnskab 1577

Øresundstoldregnskab 1578

Øresundstoldregnskab 1580

Øresundstoldregnskab 1581

Øresundstoldregnskab 1583

Øresundstoldregnskab 1585

Øresundstoldregnskab 1 May 1587-1 May 1588

Øresundstoldregnskab 1 May 1588-1 May 1589

Øresundstoldregnskab 1 May 1589-1 May 1590 (Morten Jensen)

(The 'Øresundstoldregnskaber' = Sound Toll Registers are available in
a digital edition under <www.Sound Toll Registers.nl>).


**University Library, St Andrews**

B 10/8/1 Burgh Court Book Crail 2 Oct. 1552-9 Aug. 1553

B 10/8/2 Burgh Court Book Crail 1554-1560

B 10/8/3 Burgh Court Book Crail 18 May – 2 Nov. 1556

B 10/8/4 Burgh Court Book Crail 30 Apr. 1566-10 Febr. 1568/9

B 10/8/5 Burgh Court Book Crail 7 June 1569-1 Mar. 1574/5

B 10/8/6 Burgh Court Book Crail 27 Mar. 1576-11 Nov. 1580

B 10/8/7 Burgh Court Book Crail 12 Nov. 1580-9 Apr. 1584

B 10/8/8 Burgh Court Book Crail 22 Febr. 1588/9-18 Febr.1591/2,
Dec. 1595

B 65/8/1 Burgh Court Book St Andrews End Febr. 1588/9-14 Nov. 1592


**Published sources**

*The Acts of the Parliaments of Scotland* II A.D. MCCCCXXIV- A.D.
MDLXVII ed Thomson, T, (1814, London: Printed by command
of His Majesty King George the third, in pursuance of an address of
the House of Commons of Great Britain).

*The Acts of the Parliament of Scotland III A.D. MDLXVII – A.D. MDXCII*
ed. Thomson, T, (1814, London : Printed by command of His
Majesty King George the third, in pursuance of an address of the
House of Commons of Great Britain).

*Das* älteste *Rostocker Stadtbuch etwa 1254-1273. Mit Beiträgen zur
Geschichte Rostocks im 13. Jahrhundert,* ed Thierfelder, H, (1967,
Göttingen: Vandenhoeck & Ruprecht).

*Das* älteste *Stralsundische Stadtbuch 1270-1310*, ed Fabricius, K W F, (1872, Berlin: Weber).

*Das* älteste *Wismarsche Stadtbuch von etwa 1250 bis 1272* , ed Techen, F, (1912, Wismar:Hinstorff).

Balfour, D (ed), *Oppressions of the Sixteenth Century in the Islands of Orkney and Zetland; from Original Documents*, (1859, Edinburgh: Abbotsford Club 31).

Ballantyne, J H, and Smith, B (eds), *Shetland Documents 1195-1579*, (1999, Lerwick: Shetland Islands Council & Shetland Times).

Ballantyne, J H, and Smith, B (eds), *Shetland Documents, 1580-1611*, (1994, Lerwick: Shetland Islands Council & Shetland Times).

Clouston, J S (ed), *Records of the Earldom of Orkney, 1299-1614*, Scottish History Society 2nd Series VII, (1914, Edinburgh).

Gregory, D (ed), 'Documents illustrative of the history of the fisheries in the West Highlands and Isles. Collectanea de Rebus Albanicis, consisting of original papers and documents relating to the history of the Highlands and Islands of Scotland', *Edinburgh, Iona Club*, 1847, pp 97-111.

Marwick, J D (ed), *Extracts from the Records of the Burgh of Edinburgh* V A.D. 1573-1589, (1882, Edinburgh).

M'Neill, G P (ed), *Rotuli Scaccarium Regum Scotorum, The Exchequer Rolls of Scotland XXI*, (1901, Edinburgh: Series of chronicles and memorials published by authority of the Lords Commissioners of H M Treasury under the direction of the Lord Clerk – Register of Scotland.

Miller, A H (ed) *The Compt Buik of David Wedderburne Merchant of Dundee 1587-1630. Together with the Shipping Lists of Dundee 1580-1618*, (Scottish History Society XXVIII), (1898: Edinburgh).

Mooney, J, (ed), *Charters and other records of the city and royal burgh of Kirkwall*, (1952, Aberdeen: Third Spalding Club no. 19).

*Die Recesse und andere Akten der Hansetage von 1256-1430* II ed. Koppmann, K (1872,Leipzig: Duncker & Humblot).

*Records of the Convention of the Royal Burghs of Scotland* I ed Marwick, J D, (1866, Edinburgh: W. Paterson).

*The Register of the Privy Council of Scotland* I, ed Burton, J H (1877, Edinburgh: H.M. General Register House).

*The Register of the Privy Council of Scotland* II ed Burton, J H 1878, Edinburgh: H.M. General Register House).

*The Register of the Privy Council of Scotland* III ed Masson, D, (1880, Edinburgh: H.M.General Register House).

*The Register of the Privy Council of Scotland* IV ed Masson, D, (1881, Edinburgh : H.M. General Register House).

Rehme, P, *Das Lübecker Ober-Stadtbuch. Ein Beitrag zur Geschichte der Rechtsquellen und des Liegenschaftsrechtes. Mit einem Urkundenbuche,* (1895, Hannover: Helwing).

Rogers, C (ed), *Register of the Collegiate Church of Crail with introductory remarks,* (1877, London: Grampian Club no. 15).

Secher, V A (ed), *Corpus Constitutionum Daniæ. Forordninger, Recesser og andre kongelige Breve, Danmarks Lovgivning vedkommende* I, (1887, Copenhagen: Selskabet for Udgivelse af Kilder til dansk Historie).

*Der Stralsunder Liber memorialis,* 6 vols, ed Schröder, H-D, (1964-1988, Rostock-Schwerin-Weimar: Böhlau).

Wood , M, (ed), *Court Book of the Regality of Broughton and the Burgh of the Canongate 1569-1573,* (1937, Edinburgh: Oliver and Boyd).

*Das Zweite Stralsundische Stadtbuch 1310-1342,* 2 vols, eds Reuter, C, Lietz, P and Wehner, O, (1896-1903, Stralsund: Verlag der Königlichen Regierungs-Buchdruckerei).

*Das zweite Wismarsche Stadtbuch 1272-1297. Liber vel de impignoratione vel emptione seu venditione hereditatum vel aliorum bonorum ,* 2 vols, ed Lotte Knabe unter Mitwirkung von Anneliese Düring (Quellen und Darstellungen zur Hansischen Geschichte NF XIV 1-2), (1966, Weimar: Böhlau).

## Secondary works

Anson, P F, *Fishing Boats and Fisher Folk on the East Coast of Scotland,* (1930,London-Toronto).

Baldwin, J R (ed), *Scandinavian Shetland: an Ongoing Tradition?* (1978, Edinburgh: Scottish Society for Northern Studies).

Bang-Andersen, A, Greenhill, B, and Grude, E H (eds) *The North Sea a highway of economic and cultural exchange character* (1985,Oxford: Oxford University Press).

Barrett, J H, Nicholson, R A and Cerón-Carrasco, R, 'Archaeo-ichtyological Evidence for Longterm Socioeconomic Trends in Northern Scotland: 3500 BC to AD 1500', *Journal of Archaeological Science* 26, (1999), pp 353-88.

van Bochove, C , 'The 'Golden Mountain': An Economic Analysis of Holland's Early Modern Herring Fisheries', in Sicking, L and Abreu-Ferreira, D (eds) *Beyond the Catch: Fisheries of the North Atlantic, the North Sea and the Baltic, 900-1850,* (2009, Leiden-Boston: Brill), pp 207-44.

Boissonade, P, 'Le mouvement commercial entre la France et les Iles britanniques au XVe siècle', *Revue historique* 134, (1920), pp 1-27.

Brown, C, *Scottish Regional Recipes*, (1981, Glasgow: The Molendinar Press).

Bryce, W M, 'The Burgh Muir of Edinburgh from the Records' , *The Book of the Old Edinburgh Club* 10, (1918), pp 1-263.

Comar, R D, Simpson, A D C and Morrison-Low, A D, *Weights and Measures in Scotland: a European Perspective*, (2004, East Linton: Tuckwell Press).

Coull, J R, 'Fisheries in Scotland in the 16th, 17th, and 18th Centuries: the evidence in Macfarlane's Geographical Collections', *Scottish Geographical Magazine* 93, (1977), pp 5-14.

Coull, J R, *The Sea Fisheries of Scotland. A Historical Geography*, (1996,Edinburgh: John Donald).

Coull, J R, 'The Development of Herring Fishing in the Outer Hebrides', *International Journal of Maritime History* 15,2, (2003), pp 21-42.

Coull, J R, Fenton, A and Veitch, K (eds) *Boats, Fishing and the Sea: Scottish Life and Society: A Compendium of Scottish Ethnology* IV, (2008, Edinburgh: John Donald in association with The European Ethnological Research Centre).

Devine, T M and Lythe, S G E, 'The economy of Scotland under James VI', *Scottish Historical Review* 50, (1971), pp 91-106.

*A Dictionary of the Older Scottish Tongue*... I-XII eds Craigie, W A, Aitken, A J, and Dureau, M G, (1931-2002, Chicago: University of Chicago Press (vols I-IV), Aberdeen: Aberdeen University Press (vols V-VIII), Oxford (Oxford University Press vols VIII-XII).

Farnie, H, *The Fife Coast. From Queensberry to Fifeness*, ([1861],Cupar).

Fenton, A, *The Northern Isles: Orkney and Shetland*, (1978, Edinburgh: John Donald).

Idem, *The Food of the Scots: Scottish Life and Society. A Compendium on Scottish Ethnology* V, (2007, Edinburgh: John Donald).

Fenton, A, Mackay, M A, (eds) *Scottish Life and Society. An Introduction to Scottish Ethnology, A Compendium of Scottish Ethnology* I, (2013, Edinburgh: John Donald in association with the European Ethnological Research Centre).

Fulton, T W, *The Sovereignty of the Sea. An Historical Account of the Claims of England to the Dominion of the British Seas, and of the Evolution of the Territorial Waters: with special reference to the Rights of Fishing and the Naval Salute*, (1911, Edinburgh-London: William Blackwood and Sons).

Gibson, A J S and Smout, T C, *Prices, Food and Wages in Scotland 1550-1780*, (1995, Cambridge: Cambridge University Press).

Gibson, W M, *The Herring Fishing I: Stronsay*, (1984, Edinburgh: B.P.P.).

Goodare, J, 'The long hundred in medieval and early modern Scotland', *Proceedings of the Society of Antiquaries of Scotland* 123, (1993), pp 396-418.

Goodlad, C A, *Shetland Fishing Saga*, (1971, Lerwick: Shetland Times Ltd.).

Graham, A, 'Old harbours and landing places on the east coast of Scotland', *Proceedings of the Society of Antiquaries of Scotland* 108, (1976-77), pp 332-65.

Guy, I, The Scottish Export Trade, 1460-1599, from the Exchequer Rolls, (1982, unpubl M Phil Thesis , University of St Andrews).

Eadem, 'The Scottish Export trade, 1460-1599', in: Smout, T C (ed) *Scotland and Europe, 1200-1850*, (1986, Edinburgh: John Donald), pp 62-81.

Harris, B, 'Scotland's Herring Fisheries and the Prosperity of the Nation, *c* 1660-1760', *Scottish Historical Review* 79, (2000), pp 39-60.

Hay, E R and Walker, B, *Focus on Fishing: Arbroath & Gourdon*, Abertay Historical Society Publication no. 23, (Dundee 1985: Dundee Abertay Historical Society).

Jahnke, C, *Das Silber des Meeres. Fang und Vertrieb von Ostseehering zwischen Norwegen und Italien (12.-16. Jahrhundert)*, Quellen und Darstellungen zur Hansischen Geschichte Neue Folge XLIX, (2000, Köln-Weimar-Wien: Böhlau).

LeRoy Ladurie, E, *Montaillou, village occitan de 1294 à 1324*, (1975, Paris: Gallimard).

Lillehammer, A, 'The Scottish-Norwegian Timber Trade in the Stavanger Area in the Sixteenth and Seventeenth Centuries', in Smout, T C ed., *Scotland and Europe, 1200-1850*, (1986, Edinburgh: John Donald), pp 97-111.

Idem, 'Boards, Beams and Barrel Hoops: Contacts between Scotland and the Stavanger Area in the Seventeenth Century', in Simpson, G G ed., *Scotland and Scandinavia, 800-1800*, (1990, Edinburgh: John Donald), pp 100-6.

Liszka, T R and Walker, L E M (eds) *The North Sea World in the Middle Ages: Studies in the Cultural History of North-Western Europe*, (2001, Dublin: Four Courts Press).

Lynch, M, *Edinburgh and the Reformation*, (1981, Edinburgh: John Donald).

Idem, *Scotland. A New History*, 2nd ed., (1992, London: Pimlico).

Martin, A, *The ring-net fishermen*, (1981, Edinburgh: John Donald).

Martin, C J M, 'Seafaring and Trade in East Fife', in Liszka, T R and Walker, L E M (eds) *The North Sea World in the Middle Ages: Studies in the Cultural History of North-Western Europe*, (2001, Dublin: Four Courts Press).

Michell, A R, 'The European Fisheries in Early Modern History', in Rich, E E, and Wilson, C (eds) *The Cambridge Economic History of Europe* V, (1987, Cambridge: Cambridge University Press), pp 133-84.

Murray, J E L, 'The Agriculture of Crail, 1550-1600', *Scottish Studies*, (1964), pp 85-95.

Poulsen, B, *Dutch Herring. An Environmental History, c. 1600-1860*, (2008, Amsterdam: Uitgeverij Aksant).

Riis, T, 'Navigation et formation des marins en Ecosse vers 1600', in *Horizons marins – Itinéraires spirituels (Mélanges Michel Mollat)* II eds Dubois, H, Hocquet, J C and Vauchez, A, (1987, Paris: Publications de la Sorbonne), pp 295-304.

Riis, T, *Should Auld Acquaintance Be Forgot...Scottish-Danish relations c. 1450-1707*, 2 vols, (1988, Odense: Odense University Press).

Riis, T, 'The Baltic Trade of Montrose in the Sixteenth & Seventeenth Centuries from the Danish Sound Toll Registers', in Jackson, G and Lythe, S G E (eds) *The Port of Montrose. A history of its harbour, trade and shipping* (1993, Tayport, Hutton Press), pp 102-14.

Rorke, M, 'The Scottish Herring Trade, 1470-1600', *Scottish Historical Review* 84, (2005), pp 149-65.

*The Scottish National Dictionary* I-X, eds Grant, W, and Murison, D D, (1931-76, Edinburgh: Scottish National Dictionary Association).

Shaw, F J, *The Northern and Western Islands of Scotland: Their Economy and Society in the Seventeenth Century*, (1980 Edinburgh: John Donald).

Sicking, L, 'Protection Costs and Profitability of the Herring Fishery in the Netherlands in the Sixteenth Century: A Case Study', *International Journal of Maritime History* 15,2, (2003), pp 265-77.

Sicking, L and Abreu-Ferreira, D (eds) *Beyond the Catch: Fisheries of the North Atlantic, the North Sea and the Baltic, 900-1850*, (2009, Leiden-Boston : Brill).

Simpson, G G (ed), *Scotland and Scandinavia, 800-1800*, (1990, Edinburgh: John Donald).

Idem, (ed) *Scotland and the Low Countries, 1124-1994*, (1996, East Linton: Tuckwell).

Smith, H D, *Shetland Life and Trade 1550-1914*, (1984, Edinburgh: John Donald).

Smith, P, *The Lammas Drave and the Winter Herin'. A History of the Herring Fishing from East Fife*, (1985, Edinburgh).

Smout, T C (ed) *Scotland and Europe, 1200-1850*, (1986, Edinburgh: John Donald),

Idem (ed), *Scotland and the Sea*, (1992, Edinburgh: John Donald).

Smout, T C and Stewart, M, *The Firth of Forth. An Environmental History* (2012, Edinburgh, Birlinn Limited).

Smylie, M, *Herring. A History of the Silver Darlings*, 2nd ed., (2011, Stroud: History Press).

Sutherland, I, *From Herring to Seine Net Fishing on the East Coast of Scotland*, (1985, Wick: Camps Bookshop).

Taylor, S ed. with Markus, G (eds) *The Place-Names of Fife* I-V, (2006-12, Donington: Shaun Tyas).

Tracy, J D, 'Herring Wars: the Habsburg Netherlands and the Struggle for Control of the North Sea, ca. 1520-1560', *Sixteenth Century Journal* 24, (1993), p. 249-72.

Unger, R W, 'Dutch Herring, Technology and International Trade in the Seventeenth Century', *Journal of Economic History* 40, (1980), pp 253-79.

Verlinden, C (ed), *Documents pour l'histoire des prix et des salaires en Flandre et en Brabant (XVe-XVIIIe siècle) / Dokumenten voor de Geschiedenis van prijzen en lonen in Vlaanderen en Brabant (XVe-XVIIIe eeuw)*, (1959, Bruges: De Tempel).

Whatley, C A, *'That Important and Necessary Article'. The Salt Industry and Its Trade in Fife and Tayside, c. 1570-1850*, Abertay Historical Society Publications no. 22, (1984, Dundee: Dundee Abertay Historical Society).

Idem, *The Scottish Salt Industry 1570-1850, an economic and social history*, (1987, Aberdeen: Aberdeen University Press).

Whyte, I D, *Scotland's Society and Economy in Transition, c. 1500 – c. 1700*, (1997, Basingstoke: Macmillan).

Zupko, R E, 'The Weights and Measures of Scotland before the Union', *Scottish Historical Review* 56, (1977), pp 119-45.

# Index

# D

Great Belt 56
Great Yarmouth xii
Greif, John 21, 131, 138, 140, 142, 144
Greive, John 115
Grig, David 127, 143
Grig, Edward 127, 129, 131, 137, 143, 163

## H

Hall, Thomas 46, 125, 144
Hamburg xiv, 1, 85
Hamilton, John 13, 26, 122, 144
Hamilton, Ninian 42, 67, 120, 123, 125, 131, 144, 164
Hanseatic towns xiv, 1
Harte, James 53
Harte, John 19, 23, 26, 51, 52, 61, 62, 78, 79, 121, 122, 124, 126, 128, 129, 131, 132, 133, 134, 136, 137, 144, 145, 159, 164
Hawson, David 15, 132, 142
Hawson, William 70, 125, 132, 133, 135, 138, 139, 145, 148, 151, 153
Hay, Walter 112, 160
Hebrides 14, 19, 24, 36, 37, 81, 86, 92, 178
highest market price 3, 6, 13, 14, 19, 20, 23, 42, 46, 50, 51, 52, 61, 62, 63, 74, 79, 88
Hogg, Patrick 22, 46, 51, 74, 125, 128, 130, 135, 145, 164
Holbetar, John 137, 143
Holeis, Janet 28
Howat, Thomas 49
Hudson, John, merchant of York 67
Hunter, William 6, 7, 8, 45, 51, 61, 64, 130, 132, 142, 145, 158, 160, 164

## I

Iberian Peninsula xi
Inglis, Alexander 13
Ireland 18
Isle of Skye 17
Isles (Hebrides) 13, 16, 17, 19, 20, 30, 52, 58, 63, 64, 74, 81, 85, 89, 97, 176
Italy xi

## J

James V, King of Scotland 16
Jensen, Morten, customs officer at Elsinore 100, 175
John, Bishop of the Isles 17
John, Nicol, mariner of Anstruther 22, 68

## K

Kam, William 122, 139
Kay, Agnes 9
Kay, Alexander, St Andrews 29, 30
Kay, Andro, merchant at St Andrews 66, 73
Kay, Archibald 129, 145
Kay, John 132, 152, 158, 161
Kay, Thomas 9, 67, 121, 123, 129, 137, 138, 146, 161, 164
Kay, William 4, 15, 58, 75, 78, 122, 125, 131, 132, 134, 139, 140, 141, 143, 145, 146, 151, 152, 153
Keracher, fishmonger at St Andrews 94
Kid, George 132, 142
Kiel, University Library ix
Kilrenny xvi
Kingow, John 29

128, 133, 134, 138, 139, 144,
147, 148, 151
Martin, William  134, 153
Martyn, Andrew  15
Mary of Guise  16
Mary, Queen of Scots  74, 77
Mayerton, George  120, 137
Mayerton, John  126, 145
Mayerton, Thomas  134, 145
McCall, Mungo, merchant at Edin-
burgh  76
Mediterranean  90
Meldrum, Alexander  90
Meldrum, George  57, 112, 125, 127,
134, 138, 148, 160, 165
Meldrum, James  22, 120, 132, 135,
136, 148, 166
Melville, Andrew  16
Melville, Andrew, younger  71, 134,
148
Melville, Andro  73, 134, 148, 160,
166
Melville, John  71, 73, 120, 123, 125,
127, 129, 134, 135, 140, 142, 153
Melville, John, elder  4, 5, 16, 54, 60,
71, 72, 78
Melville, John, younger  19, 71, 72,
148, 166
Melville/Melvyne, John, elder  158,
166
Melville/Melvyne, John, younger  158
Melville, William  50, 66, 121, 128,
129, 130, 149, 166
Mercer, John  13
Mertene, John  20
Mertyne, Thomas  25
Migrations of herring  xi
Millar, Peter  88
Minch, the  17
Monipenny, James  20, 25, 126, 149

Monipenny, William  128, 149
Montaillou (France)  81, 108, 180
Moray  76
Moreis, Thomas  36
Morris, Andrew  13
Morrison, Thomas  135, 146
Morris, Robert  62, 134, 149, 153
Morris, Thomas  22, 135, 143, 145,
152
Morton  72
Morton, Earl of, Regent  77
Morton, George  149
Morton, John  4, 5, 56, 60, 61, 72, 88
Morton, Robert  72
Morton, William  2, 28, 51, 52, 61,
62, 63, 72, 120, 123, 124, 125,
126, 128, 130, 131, 132, 134,
135, 137, 149
Muyr, Robert  135, 152
Myrton, John  6, 61, 71
Myrton, Thomas  127, 150

# N

Napier, William  76, 77, 150
National Archives of Scotland  ix, xv,
xvi, 31, 173
National Library of Scotland  ix
Netherlands  xi, 85, 86, 181, 182
Newcastle  18
Nicoll, James  127, 150
Northern Germany  1
Northern Isles  xiv, 7, 11, 13, 14, 19,
24, 36, 37, 81, 115, 179
Northern Scotland  2, 12, 16, 17, 18,
19, 20, 21, 24, 25, 26, 27, 30, 32,
33, 35, 39, 49, 50, 51, 52, 53, 58,
62, 63, 64, 65, 67, 68, 71, 72, 74,
79, 81, 85, 93, 115, 117, 178
North Sea  xi, 48, 59, 70, 85, 90, 96,

178, 180, 181, 182
Norway vii, x, xiv, 3, 4, 5, 6, 31, 37,
47, 48, 57, 58, 59, 60, 61, 63, 69,
70, 72, 73, 76, 81, 83, 89, 105,
115, 156, 158, 159, 162, 166

# O

Obondis, William 135, 151
Oliphant, Christine 65, 121, 136,
150, 166
Øresundstoldregnskaber 119, 175
Orkney xiii, xiv, 11, 12, 14, 19, 85,
97, 176, 179
Orphal, J xvi
Ottar, John 62, 135, 149
Ottar, Robert 62, 135, 149, 153

# P

Page, David 62, 126, 132, 136, 150
Paisley Abbey 76
Parkie, John 6, 134, 153
Parliament of Scotland 88, 175
Partie, John 61
Paterson, John 51, 131, 135, 145,
148, 153
Paterson, John, of Crail 26
Paterson, John, of Pittenweem 12
Paterson, Thomas 77, 112, 113
Patie, Thomas, younger 135, 148
Payson, Andro 135, 138
Peirson, Andrew, Andro 15, 45, 59,
126, 144, 146
Peirson, George 4, 21, 22, 32, 37,
55, 60, 62, 68, 72, 135, 136, 142,
143, 145, 148, 154, 158
Peterhead 22
Pittenweem xiv, xvi, 3, 12, 22, 23, 31,
46, 47, 48, 95, 97, 98, 100, 101,

102, 103, 105, 106, 110, 120,
154, 159, 168, 173, 174
Customs Accounts 31
placeDundee 129
Portugal xi
Powsta, William 73, 126, 150, 166
Powstey, William 128
Prestonpans 46, 74, 124, 125, 127,
129, 130, 132, 134, 136, 144,
151, 167
Prussia 1
Pyrenees 81

# Q

Queen's Men 74, 75, 78

# R

Ramsay, Alexander, merchant at Dun-
dee 46, 47, 67, 112, 160, 165
Ramsay, John 135, 151
Ramsay, Thomas, customs officer at
Crail 111
Reid, Alexander 74, 124, 127, 129,
130, 132, 134, 136, 144, 151, 167
Reid, John 74, 75, 90, 121, 132, 136,
139, 143, 151, 154
Reid, John, elder 136, 139
Reid, John, younger 121, 139
Robertson, Andro 160
Robertson, Thomas 8, 136, 151
Robertson, William 52, 53, 136, 145
Rostock xiv, xv, 1, 87, 177
Rouen 72, 73, 134, 140
Ruthven regime 75
Ryd, John 7

# V

Vtyng, David 29

# W

Wade, James, in Lambieletham 7
Walker, John 88
Walker, William 9
Watson, Charles 135, 152
Welwood, John 74, 128, 131, 153, 168
Welwood, Thomas 65, 74, 122, 135, 153, 168
Wemyss, Alexander 137, 143
Wemyss, John 72, 78, 112, 132, 134, 153, 168
Wemyss, Thomas 9
Western Isles 8, 12, 17, 19, 20, 23, 24, 36, 37
West Indies 90
White, Henry 137, 152
Wiggan, Thomas 159
Williamson, James 134, 153
Wilson, Andro 137, 138, 143, 146
Wilson, James 29
Wilson, John 137, 143, 147, 149, 150, 154, 159, 160, 161
Wilson, John, elder 161
Wilson, John, huikmaker 137
Wilson, John, seaman 137
Wishart, Archibald 74, 122, 124, 128, 153, 168
Wismar xv, 87, 176
Witkow, John 137, 152
Woed, Alexander 62, 149
Woede, Alexander 65, 67, 68, 137, 144, 146
Woede, James 120, 153
Woede, James, elder 168

Woede, James, younger 168
Woede, Ninian 124, 129, 131, 135, 153, 168
Woed, Ninian 121, 136
Woed, William 138, 139
Woid, Andro 53
Woide, James 129
Woide, Ninian 23
Woid, James 51, 53, 120, 131, 136, 154
Woid, Ninian 52, 53, 120, 136, 137

# Y

Young, Janet 66, 121, 134, 136, 154, 168
Young, William 138, 140, 148

# Z

Zuiderzee 1

Lightning Source UK Ltd.
Milton Keynes UK
UKOW06f1646041116
286880UK00002B/46/P